TL146.5 C37 2004

edited by
The car and its future.

The
Reference
Shelf®

The Car and Its Future

Edited by Kaitlen Jay Exum and Lynn M. Messina

LIBRARY
CAMDEN COUNTY COLLEGE
BLACKWOOD, NJ

WITHDRAWN

The Reference Shelf
Volume 76 • Number 5

The H. W. Wilson Company
2004

The Reference Shelf

The books in this series contain reprints of articles, excerpts from books, addresses on current issues, and studies of social trends in the United States and other countries. There are six separately bound numbers in each volume, all of which are usually published in the same calendar year. Numbers one through five are each devoted to a single subject, providing background information and discussion from various points of view and concluding with a subject index and comprehensive bibliography that lists books, pamphlets, and abstracts of additional articles on the subject. The final number of each volume is a collection of recent speeches, and it contains a cumulative speaker index. Books in the series may be purchased individually or on subscription.

Library of Congress has cataloged this title as follows:

The car and its future / edited by Kaitlen Jay Exum and Lynn M. Messina.
     p. cm.—(The reference shelf; v. 76, no. 5)
   Includes bibliographical references and index.
   ISBN 0-8242-1037-9
   1. Automobiles—Design and construction. 2. Automobile industry and trade—Forecasting. 3. Automobiles—Technological innovations. 4. Highway engineering—Technological innovations. I. Exum, Kaitlen Jay. II. Messina, Lynn M. III. Series.

TL146.5.C37 2004
629.222—dc22
                                                       2004048908

On the cover: The Smart 600 Pulse Softouch, at the 2003 Frankfurt Auto Show. Courtesy of Michael A. Messina.

Copyright © 2004 by the H.W. Wilson Company. All rights reserved. No part of this work may be reproduced or copied in any form or by any means, including but not restricted to graphic, electronic, and mechanical—for example, photocopying, recording, taping, or information and retrieval systems—without the express written permission of the publisher, except that a reviewer may quote and a magazine, newspaper, or electronic information service may print brief passages as part of a review written specifically for inclusion in that magazine, newspaper, or electronic service.

Visit H.W. Wilson's Web site: www.hwwilson.com

Printed in the United States of America

Contents

Preface

One out of every two Americans owns a car. For the approximately 1.8 million households in the United States, there are 1.9 million automobiles; a mere 8 percent of households do not own cars. The United States is the largest market of automobile consumers in the world. It is safe to say that Americans love their cars. They like what they have now, they're excited about upcoming models, and they wait breathlessly for the cars of the future, hoping that they will get incredible mileage, produce no emissions, and, ultimately, fly like Chitty Chitty Bang Bang.

To a certain extent, Americans' infatuation with cars makes sense. In a country as large as the United States, cars are often a veritable necessity. Many people, provided they do not live in one of the few American cities with extensive public transportation, need cars for their daily commutes and their vacations. Cars allow people to travel from the suburbs to the city and back again, to navigate the ever spreading urban sprawl. However, there is more to this love affair with cars than simple practicality. Cars are the stuff of fantasy; for proof, look at the litany of films and music that reference, even idealize vehicles. Disney's *Herbie, the Love Bug* starred a Volkswagen Beetle with personality. Michael J. Fox relied on a DeLorean, complete with gull wings and mythical flux capacitor, to take him *Back to the Future*. And such films as *Grease* and *American Graffiti* sparked a resurgence in interest in 1950s car culture and the phenomenon of cruising. Such songs as the Beach Boys' "Little Deuce Coupe" and Prince's "Little Red Corvette" only furthered the obsession.

Without a doubt, the United States is a car culture, and Americans want it all: safety, glamour, mileage, and that elusive "coolness factor." Today's autos can accelerate to illegal speeds, and suburbanites who use their vehicles only for errands own sport utility vehicles (SUVs) with off-road capabilities. Admittedly, sometimes a driver's wants are frivolous, but not always. There is an increasingly persuasive drive toward eco-conscious vehicles that run on alternative fuels like hydrogen fuel cells, diesel, and electricity. Hybrids, or cars with both gasoline engines and electric motors, are the new big thing; whether or not they have staying power remains to be seen. Also popular are tiny autos like the Smart Car and the BMW Mini Cooper, both of which tend to be inexpensive and get good mileage.

Another trend is toward light trucks and SUVs. The Hummer, popularized by actor-turned–California governor Arnold Schwarzenegger, is the paragon of the bigger-is-better trend. While such vehicles get notoriously poor mileage per gallon, many drivers feel safer wrapped in tons of steel and reassured by four-wheel drive.

So, which vehicle will win the war, the massive SUV or the minuscule car? Maybe neither, since there has been an upsurge in the popularity of sports cars, too. Since the global market for cars continues to grow (especially gaining speed in China), perhaps there is room for all these cars. If vehicles are engaged in a large-scale popularity contest, then Generation Y may very well have the power to decide the winner. Carmakers and insurance companies are actively gearing their products to Generation Y, a force approximately 63 million strong, even though many of them cannot even drive yet. Known for not wanting to feel as if they are being marketed to, members of Generation Y present an elusive market to be cracked. Automakers and insurers are targeting them through teen-oriented print ads, television commercials, and Web sites; whether such tactics work will be seen only after Generation Y comes into its own buying power.

When we consider car production rather than purchasing power, in some respects Europe and the United States have become passé. Asia is taking over the market, not only with plants in such countries as Japan and Korea but with Asian-owned factories in North America. Honda and Toyota are two companies at the forefront of hybrid production; they are responsible for the Civic and Insight and the Prius, respectively.

The Car and Its Future considers automobiles and automotive technologies from a variety of angles. The book's first chapter examines how people feel about and use their cars, including how they drive, methods of car shopping, and purchasing habits. The next chapter looks at the psychology of vehicle design, the effects of manufacturing techniques on quality, and the high technology that goes into our cars. The following chapter considers safety issues, including accident rates, driving techniques that compromise the safety of all drivers, the issue of child safety, and the psychology of driving. The auto insurance industry is the topic of the next chapter, which looks at the best way to obtain reasonably priced insurance as well as at the relationships between insurers and repair shops. Another chapter covers the automotive industry from a global perspective, including foreign car manufacturing in the United States, the effects of America's foreign policy on gas prices and the auto industry, and the state of car manufacturing in Europe and Asia. The final chapter considers vehicles that use alternative fuels, including hybrid cars and those that run on hydrogen, electricity, and diesel, exploring how environmentally friendly they are and how soon they can be successfully mass-marketed.

We would like to thank the many periodical publishers who have so generously granted permission to reprint their articles in these pages. We also must express our gratitude to those at the H. W. Wilson Company who helped to produce and research this book, especially Sandra Watson and Jennifer Peloso, as well as Michael A. Messina, who graciously donated his photographs. Thanks also to Gray Young, Rich Stein, Norris Smith, and Clifford Thompson.

Kaitlen Jay Exum
Lynn M. Messina
October 2004

I. Life Behind the Wheel

Editors' Introduction

Americans alone drive 1.6 trillion miles a year. That adds up to an awful lot of time in the car, so when they decide to invest in some transportation, they consider a number of factors. Do they want to own the car, or just lease? Is there an advantage to buying online, or do they need to sit in the car, feel the upholstery, kick the tires? How large a vehicle do they need? Which extras can they simply not live without? Anyone who expects to sit in traffic for several hours a day wants to be comfortable and make sure that the automobile is outfitted with all the luxuries and conveniences of home. Commuters especially want all the amenities, packed into one safe car that makes them look cool. Then they have to get realistic.

In "Going Through the Emotions," Jim Mueller explains how sometimes buyers need to forgo their dream cars in order to choose vehicles that are practical. In some cases, the dream car and the practical option are one and the same; just as often, they are not. Mueller discusses how buyers—particularly those most optimistic of shoppers: first-time buyers—must reconcile their emotions with logic in the course of the hunt for the ideal car.

Before taking home any auto, consumers first need to decide whether to lease or buy. Julie Blacklidge sorts out some of the confusion in "Lease/Buy? Auto Deals Not So Easy." She stresses that there is no one answer to the buy-or-lease conundrum and urges those in the market for a car to look at each deal on an individual basis and calculate the costs involved before making a decision.

If consumers do decide to buy their vehicles, they might refer to Bob Keefe's article, "Online Car Sales Gaining Speed After Slow Start," which documents the gaining popularity of buying cars over the Internet. Companies such as Autobytel Inc. and Autotrader.com have finally become profitable after, respectively, seven and five years online, and eBay Motors reached profitability almost immediately after its launch three years ago. Consumers have steadily been disproving skeptics who maintain that shoppers need to see and test-drive cars before making purchases; many individuals who have bought their vehicles online boast of the ease, convenience, and thrift of their Internet transactions.

Another important transaction, whether it is made online or in person, involves what type of car is appropriate for young drivers. In "Go for a Sedan for Teen's First Car, Experts Say," Amanda Rogers tackles the issue of how to best protect new drivers who, through lack of experience, are likely to be involved in accidents. The verdict: buy teens large, heavy cars with low centers of gravity. When choosing cars for themselves, shoppers might consider renting, as Jaquetta White suggests in "Just Taking a Spin." By renting a variety of vehicles, drivers can test-drive cars they might want to buy in the future, use a flashier vehicle to drive to a special event, or simply avoid racking up mileage on their own cars. It is not a common tactic, but it is becoming a definite trend.

Something else that is gaining prevalence is the SUV debate. Some drivers swear by their SUVs, citing them as spacious and safe, whereas others denounce them as environmentally unfriendly, gas-guzzling, road-hogging monsters. In this polarizing debate, outlined by Peter Roff and Jillian Jonas in "R.I.P. SUVs?" the two sides that have emerged are epitomized by the light truck–driving suburban family, complete with kids and car pools, and the fans of smaller, more fuel-efficient cars, who consider SUVs menaces and blame them for the United States' dependence on foreign oil. Although light trucks are not known to be fuel-efficient, as Gregory Cancelada points out in "Drivers Stick with Light Trucks Despite Heavy Fuel Prices," many SUV drivers consistently defend their vehicles, despite the increasing cost of filling their tanks.

Going Through the Emotions

By Jim Mueller
Chicago Tribune, July 10, 2003

Removing the emotional element of buying a car is a touchy subject with auto dealers, and understandably so. After all, emotion plays a crucial role in new-and used-car sales, and dealers are in business to sell cars.

Something triggers the impulse to shop, and that's fine in the experienced consumer who's been through the car-buying wars.

But what about the first-time buyer?

Erwin Weil, owner of Weil Cadillac-Hummer in Libertyville, has sold cars in the Chicago area for 45 years and doesn't see many first-timers at his upscale agency. But there was a time when he owned a used-car operation on Western Avenue near Lane Technical High School in Chicago and dealt with young folks all agog about buying first cars.

"Would I try to talk a young woman out of a certain car if she had her heart set on it?" asked Weil. "No. She'd buy the same car somewhere down the street, and I'd lose a sale and nothing would be solved.

"You need to be careful, because cars are an extension of our personalities. You can't step on somebody's dream. When I had the Western Avenue lot, I would talk with younger buyers to learn exactly what they needed. But I wouldn't tell a kid not to buy a specific car. I might make an attempt to taper or shape a sale if I felt he was unsure of his budget or whatever. I'd show options and ask, 'Would this one work for you just as well?'"

Sometimes he had help. Weil remembered one teenage boy coming in with his parents, determined to buy a muscle car, "and acting really out of line, I thought. I sat there and listened, and it was obvious his parents didn't want him to have the car. He was quite upset. He said, 'If you don't let me have this car, I'm gonna go buy a motorcycle and kill myself!' It was childish, where his head was at. But what could I do? I sat there and let his parents handle the situation, and he didn't buy the car."

Wijdan Zapata, a Chicago medical secretary, said she could have used an Erwin Weil 15 years ago when, at 22, she went shopping for her first dream car—a 16-valve 1988 Volkswagen Jetta GLI.

Zapata initially checked out one dealership. At the last minute, though, something told her to take along her two older brothers for moral support.

Article by Jim Mueller from the *Chicago Tribune* July 10 2003. Copyright © *Chicago Tribune*. Reprinted with permission.

"Oh, the salesman was obnoxious." she recalled. "He saw me coming. He could read it in my eyes. It was all over my face. I wanted that Jetta—right then. I didn't care how much I had to spend. I just wanted the car.

"My brother Sam kept pushing me away, toward the door, saying, 'Come on, let's look at other places. I'll bet we find the same car for a better price.' Sam was right. The next night we walked into [another dealership], and the exact same Jetta was there for $1,500 less than the first dealer. The same car with the same options. I still remember what I paid. It was $15,000, and it was a stretch for my budget. But I had my freedom and a very fast, very sharp car with a stick shift. I really wanted the stick!"

There was a time when the neighborhood banker might have had advice for rookie shoppers such as Zapata, but those days are mostly gone, according to Don Fisher, president of the Community Bank of Glen Ellyn/Wheaton.

Fisher, who has been writing loans for 40-plus years, has seen a fundamental change in the way most people finance automobiles, with banks involved in fewer of the transactions.

Zero-percent financing packages offered by manufacturers and home-equity lines of credit have taken the place of the savings-and-loan car note.

"I see parents using home-equity lines," Fisher said of financing for first-time buyers. "That's happened over the last five or six years. It's very common. They'll put the son or daughter's car on the home-equity line and deduct the interest, and the kids make payments to them. The exception is when parents want to help a son or daughter establish credit and they'll co-sign on an automobile loan.

"Cars are such an emotional choice," Fisher said. "A young person comes in with his heart set on a Camaro; he doesn't want to hear me say he should buy a Neon instead.

"My first question is always, 'Did you already sign a contract?' If the answer's yes, it was a good deal. Every deal that's been finalized is a good deal. We find a way to work with it."

Credit Considerations

But if the buyer hasn't made a commitment in writing, Fisher will often suggest completing a credit score.

The buyer considers income and liabilities, then figures the amount of available credit. "A credit score gives a better idea of how much you can realistically afford," he said.

Fisher said his bank typically works with Equifax and Trans Union to obtain credit scores.

Data are submitted and your credit score reflects an analysis of anything in your background that might indicate risk. How much credit you already have, your bill payment history, length of time on job, length of time at your residence, how much you owe, your net worth, income and monthly expenses.

A buyer is given points in each of these areas, and others.

There is an industry scoring formula.

A credit score of 800+ is sterling. Average folk come down in the 700s.

Younger buyers who haven't had credit established for a lengthy period and who haven't been in the work force for more than a couple of years have lower credit scores. In marginal cases a lender might ask to see another year's tax return or evidence that you're not carrying huge balances on all of your credit cards before writing a loan.

"But again, cars are an emotional purchase and that doesn't only apply to young people," Fisher said. "A few years ago I bought a [Chevrolet] Corvette. I traded in my motorcycle. I'd always wanted a Corvette. I owned my Corvette for two years and drove it maybe 2,100 miles, and got it out of my system. Now I have a Ford F-150 Lightning I drive in warm weather. Same emotions."

"Everyone's excited about buying a car," said Dan Johnston, Central Region vice president for CarMax. "I don't care if it's a minivan

---

"Price is a big part of the anxiety for many first-time [car] buyers."—**Dan Johnston, Central Region vice president, CarMax**

---

or a Corvette. We don't try to minimize excitement. You should be excited, but not anxious, and price is a big part of the anxiety for many first-time buyers.

"What we're finding is that most have pre-shopped online and already have a good idea of what they're looking for when they arrive," Johnston said. "They've seen our posted prices. They understand our policy. There is no negotiating. And we don't have a finance guy. Our financing is a la carte. We have several banks we work with, and it's a matter of the sales consultant putting in the numbers and then waiting for their responses. Buyers seem more comfortable working with the same person all the way through.

"We try to help the first-time buyer target the right vehicle. Why this particular car? What features do you need? Have you considered similar models?"

Trading in a Dream

CarMax-type options and Internet shopping weren't available in January 1983, when Lynn Janulis, a patent agent with a Chicago law firm, fell for a low-mileage 1979 Triumph TR7 on a used-car lot.

"Oh, it was totally emotional—not sensible at all," she said. "I loved the style and the whole British thing. Plus it was unique and cool, and it was blue. I took my friend Barb with me to test drive the Triumph, because I didn't even know how to drive a stick. I bought it and she drove it home and taught me that night how to drive it."

Two years later, after three snapped accelerator cables, a blown head gasket and multiple skirmishes with "a horrible electrical system and [retractable] headlights that stuck all the time," Janulis traded in her TR7 for a new Volkswagen GTI she'd drive 200,000 miles in 15 years.

The GTI was sensible, dependable. But not the same emotional investment as the TR7.

"I'd buy the Triumph again," she said. "It was a blast. I always talk fondly about the TR7. A great little car despite all my problems. The insurance was too costly. Everything about it was too costly— but it was so cool, fun and different."

And too emotional?

"Oh yeah, totally emotional. And utterly irrational."

Tips for the First-Time Buyers

David Cole is president of the Center for Automotive Research in Ann Arbor, Mich., and a veteran observer of industry trends. While acknowledging the emotional element in buying a car, he was quick to emphasize differences in the market from a generation ago.

"In the 1950s and '60s, Americans had 100 cars to choose from," Cole explained, "whereas now it's closer to 1,400.

"In terms of affordability, the real price of cars has fallen as wages have expanded. Ten years ago, we said it took 30 weeks of wages to buy the typical new car. Now we're down to 20 weeks. That increased affordability means buyers stretch to buy more car— because they can, and cars are indeed an emotional purchase," Cole said.

As for young people and first cars, Cole noted three points:

- Younger buyers are more independent in 2003 and have higher expectations. When swarmed and pressured by pushy sales associates, they're apt to turn around and leave. "They know they can walk—and they do," Cole said.

- Younger buyers often make use of the Internet. "They're cruising the world of autos—price shopping, looking at accessories. They know exactly what they want and what they'll pay for a package."

- There are two types of buyers: Those who view a car as an appliance and those who see it as a fashion statement. "You don't drive a car—you wear it!" laughed Cole. "The young person who views a car as a style statement—he's the preferred customer. But even with the appliance buyer there's an emotional element. You're writing a big check. This is a long-term obligation for most people."

Lease/Buy? Auto Deals Not So Easy

BY JULIE BLACKLIDGE
FORT WORTH BUSINESS PRESS, JUNE 6–12, 2003

Incentives to buy new cars are hard to resist.

Whether it's cash back rebates, zero percent financing, zero down, or straight leasing, the benefits and negatives to each can be confusing. An option that may be right for one consumer could end up costing another thousands of dollars.

Zero percent financing has given more consumers the opportunity to buy brand new vehicles, but industry professionals don't always recommend taking that incentive over a lease or the cash back rebate that is offered by a manufacturer.

For example, if a consumer were to buy a $45,000 car and pay it off over the full-term of the contract, generally 60 months, then that person would benefit from the zero percent finance rates. But if that same person were to pay off the note in just three years, it would have been more beneficial to lease the car, or take the rebate at the time of purchase.

"Zero percent on new cars is not really zero percent," said Jeff Crawford, general sales manager with RLB Leasing. "You have to give up a cash rebate to get that deal. So they are essentially paying $3,000 or more for the same vehicle. A lot of people would be better off with a lease. It's important to run the numbers; you have to do the math."

Will Churchill, new car sales assistant manager with Frank Kent Cadillac Oldsmobile, said when he bought his new truck he took the $3,000 rebate because he knew he only wanted the car for three years. "With zero percent financing, I would have only saved $1,500," he said.

There are several factors that should be considered before signing any sort of contract—leasing or financing—according to Churchill.

"Every customer is different," he said. "If your dealer does not ask these questions, run."

First, how many miles will be driven each year? That is essential when deciding whether to lease or buy, he said. A lease has very strict per year mileage limits. Second, will the car be used for business? If so, then a lease might be the best option because it can be used as a tax deduction. What is that consumer's churn rate? If a person likes to exchange vehicles every two years and drives 20,000 miles a year, then a purchase would the best option.

Reprinted with permission of the *Fort Worth Business Press*.

But those questions are just the beginning. There are other financial factors that must be considered. Leased vehicles require higher insurance liability limits. Leased vehicles also are subject to personal property tax in Texas, which could run as high as $800 a year, said Lori Biggs, finance manager with Frank Kent.

> *"There's no such thing as needing to put money down on a car."*—Jeff Crawford, RLB Leasing

General Motors introduced what it calls a Smart Buy, which is similar to a lease with several enhancements. One of the most glaring is that with a Smart Buy, the vehicle is titled in the individual's name rather than the finance company, cutting personal property taxes and liability insurance limits, Biggs said. At the end of both a lease and Smart Buy, the individual has an option to buy the vehicle. If the purchase is made with a Smart Buy, the sales tax already is paid. With a lease, sales tax is added on a second time.

Zero percent financing has affected leasing volumes across the country, according to Tom Libby, director of industry analysis with Power Information Network, an affiliate of J. D. Power and Associates.

"There is a strong inverse correlation between the two data sets [zero percent financing vs. leasing]; as one goes up, the other consistently goes down and vice versa," he said.

Based on the data compiled by PIN, which is gathered from over 6,000 auto franchises nationally, there is a spike upward for financing and a drastic downward spike for leases when the zero percent option is in effect. In October 2001, just after 9/11, zero percent financing sales spiked from just under 15 percent to close to 30 percent of finance transactions. Lease transactions dropped from about 18 percent to 13 percent.

April 2003 ratios are not so wide, but still show a similar trend. Zero percent transactions increased from 10 percent to nearly 20 percent by the end of the month. Leases dwindled to 14 percent from 18 percent.

Zero down is another big draw for consumers, but is also misleading, RLB's Crawford said.

"Zero down is simply just old-timey advertising; dealers use it because it sounds good," Crawford said. "The most foolish thing to do right now is put money down on a car."

He said with the zero percent financing option, consumers are better off leaving their money in a bank where it is compounding three percent interest, rather than using it to pay for a large purchase. "You're really throwing money away in that case," he said.

Churchill agreed. "You can get a higher return on your money than having it work in a mutual fund," he said.

Banks generally will finance the full amount of the vehicle and then some, Crawford said. "There's no such thing as needing to put money down on a car; most people come in here $1,500 to $5,000 upside down and we can even get that balance rolled over on top of the new loan."

For many dealers, the biggest hit to business is not the decrease in leases, but the effect zero percent financing has had on pre-owned car sales.

"Zero percent has affected the used-car market because everyone is turning in their '01s and '02s for 2003s at zero percent," Churchill said. "So you've got this gluttony of vehicles on the used car market and the value of those cars are going down. People can go out and buy a new car and get a cheaper payment than if they bought a used car."

A lower payment, however, does not necessarily mean a better deal or better value, dealers say.

Crawford said many consumers don't realize that after buying a brand new car, thousands of dollars are lost to depreciation the first year. He said people could be better off financially buying or leasing a used car—a 2002 or 2001 version of the same model.

In addition, the "residual" makes the difference, he said. A residual is the value that is set at the end of the lease term. The residual is set by the banking institution and each vehicle has a different residual value. A Mercedes Benz may have a 50 percent residual in four years, meaning it is worth 50 percent of its original value, while a Jaguar may have a 42 percent residual value. So even if both cars are priced the same, the Mercedes would have the better financial value in the long-term.

"On a new car lease, that residual is based off the new car sticker price," he said. "On the used car, the one-year old for example, it's already lost that $15,000, so your residual is $15,000 less."

Leasing used cars valued at less than $20,000 is not recommended by Crawford. He said in that case, purchasing the vehicle would be a smarter move.

The advantage to leasing a used car gets greater the more expensive the car, he said.

"If we looked at a $12,000 car, leasing doesn't give you any advantage," he said. "If you financed for 60 months your payments would be about $220. I mean how much lower would you want it?"

The average price of a used car today is over $20,000—those numbers are still workable, he said. Crawford recently negotiated a used Corvette valued at about $30,000. Because the purchaser leased the vehicle instead of financing, Crawford said he is saving $100 a month.

"It's a weird industry," Churchill said. "How you buy a car changes every month depending on incentives that are out there and the way the manufacturers are pushing them your way. You really need an educated person to help crunch numbers and figure out what is best for you. The convenient purchase may not be the right purchase."

Online Car Sales Gaining Speed After Slow Start

By Bob Keefe
Palm Beach Post (Florida), March 10, 2003

Darren Smith has bought antique swords, amber from South America and even a mummy's sarcophagus on eBay, the online bazaar.

So when Smith wanted to buy a used car, he shunned traditional auto dealers and turned to—where else—eBay.

In October, the real estate entrepreneur from the New York City borough of Staten Island bought a 1994 Chevrolet Suburban from a Dallas dealership that advertised it on the Internet auction site.

The $7,997 he paid for the SUV was about $4,000 less than the market price at the time, Smith said. Even counting an $800 shipping fee, that made his first online car purchase well worth it.

He never actually saw the Suburban before buying it. But "it got here exactly how it had been described," said Smith, 34, the owner of an Internet real estate site who knows his way around the Web. "It was a great transaction. There's no doubt in my mind this is the way I'll buy my next car."

After more starts and stops than a Ford with a bad carburetor, the Internet auto business is finally starting to hum, driven by renewed interest from people like Smith.

Last month, industry pioneer Autobytel Inc. reported its first quarterly profit after seven years of losses.

Autotrader.com became profitable in June after about five years on the Web. Today, the Atlanta-based company has more than 2.2 million used car listings on its site, more than any other Internet site.

And eBay Motors, launched by an e-commerce giant with a powerful infrastructure and millions of daily visitors, reached profitability almost immediately after leaving the starting line three years ago. Last year, it handled more than $3 billion in sales—everything from cars to brake drums and axles—accounting for about 30 percent of all eBay transactions. A car, part or accessory sells every few seconds on the site.

"We're scaling really nicely now," said Stephanie Tilenius, general manager of eBay Motors. "We're on a pretty fast track for growth."

But what a long, rough road it's been for Web-based auto sales.

Article by Bob Keefe from the *Palm Beach Post* March 10, 2003. Copyright © Cox Newspapers. Reprinted with permission.

In the 1990s, dot-com entrepreneurs bragged that they'd put traditional auto dealers out of business and revolutionize the way people bought cars. Internet shoppers, they promised, could avoid the high-pressure sales tactics, the ambiguous pricing and all the other hassles of car shopping by simply logging on, picking out their options and waiting for their car to be delivered.

Venture capitalists pumped millions of dollars into outfits like Austin, Texas-based Carorder.com, only to see their investments disappear when the companies crashed and burned. Because of everything from state laws that prohibit direct car sales by out-of-state companies to the reluctance by many shoppers to buy before kicking the tires, the industry hit the skids.

The companies that survived didn't rely on sales commissions, like the early auto sites tried to do.

Some, like eBay, make money by charging a fee for used car listings—$40 for most ads, plus another $40 when a vehicle sells.

Others, such as Autobytel and Carsdirect.com, offer new car finding services for customers and get referral fees of $25 or so from dealers in exchange for each potential sales lead.

Still others, such as Autotrader.com, make money from used car ad listings, just like newspapers make money from classified ads. About 8,000 dealers who work with Autotrader.com, for instance, pay the company $700 to $2,500 a month to list their entire inventory on the site with photos and other features.

Another 32,000 dealers are satisfied with basic listings they get as part of Autotrader.com's relationship with wholesale car auction company Manheim Auctions.

Autotrader.com and Manheim are both owned by Atlanta-based Cox Enterprises Inc., which also owns *The Palm Beach Post* and *Palm Beach Daily News*.

"Our bread and butter, our meat and potatoes is being the matchmaker between the buyer and the seller," said Autotrader.com Chief Executive Chip Perry.

While the online auto sites offer private person-to-person sales, all of them depend primarily on traditional dealers for revenues.

"Dealers are the only people that sell cars," said Autobytel Chief Executive Jeffrey Schwartz. "Internet sites don't sell cars. Manufacturers don't sell cars. Dealers have been and always will be the center of the new car selling universe."

While sites such as Autobytel and Carsdirect.com that specialize in new cars are gaining traction, it is the used car market that's poised for the most growth. Partly, that's because about 43 million used cars are sold each year, compared with an estimated 17 million new cars.

"From the new car standpoint, the jury's still out," said Kevin Prouty, an analyst with tech research firm AMR Research Inc. "Nobody thought people would be selling used cars online . . . but they are."

Setting up a showdown in the used car Internet mark Autotrader.com and eBay late last year ended a 2-1/2-year re tionship. Almost immediately, Autotrader.com launched an a tion service like eBay's.

Autotrader.com is betting used car buyers will always want to see, touch and drive the cars they want to buy, so its focus is on linking buyers in a particular ZIP code to dealers in their neighborhood.

> *Regardless of how the sites work, consumers can benefit greatly.*

EBay, on the other hand, is betting that many buyers are willing to buy a car after just looking at a picture of it, no matter where it is. More than 75 percent of all cars sold on eBay are interstate transactions.

"Some of it is all about the joy of discovery and the adventure of it," said Tilenius, head of eBay Motors.

Regardless of how the sites work, consumers can benefit greatly.

Valerie Bird estimates she saved thousands on a new $35,000 Toyota Sequoia she bought last year using Carsdirect.com. The service linked the Westerville, Ohio, woman with a Kentucky car dealership that offered the same type of car but for $7,000 less than a local dealer had.

"I wanted a color that wasn't readily available, I didn't want to wait 60 days to get it and I got it for cheaper than I would have otherwise," Bird said.

The biggest beneficiaries of the online auto services, ironically enough, may be the traditional car dealers who once feared the sites.

That's because for dealers, Internet auto sites offer an advertising and referral opportunity that can be much cheaper than traditional outlets.

Using primarily traditional media, such as newspapers, television and radio, dealers spent an average of almost $400 per car sold for advertising in 2001, according to the National Automobile Dealers Association.

By comparison, the ad cost per car for Internet advertising on eBay and Autotrader.com is less than $100, according to the companies.

"Our rates are so low that traditional newspapers, radio, television can't compete," Perry said. One of the reasons Cox Enterprises invested heavily in Autotrader.com was to diversify its offerings to advertisers beyond its newspapers, television and cable businesses.

That said, Internet companies still get only a relatively small portion of car dealers' ad budgets.

Newspapers got about 53 percent of all new car dealers' ad dollars in 2001, followed by television at almost 15 percent and radio at almost 14 percent, according to the auto dealers association. Car dealers spent less than 5 percent of their ad budgets on Internet advertising in 2001.

The Players

A sampling of online auto sales sites and how they work:

eBaymotors.com

- Owner: eBay Inc.
- How it works: Sellers pay fees—$40 upfront and $40 at the time of sale—to list used cars. Buyers can search for specific cars and bid on them auction-style.
- The good: You can also search for parts and accessories. EBay, the online auction leader, is full-featured and reliable.
- The bad: Can't search by ZIP codes, which makes it tough to find cars in just your town. Dealer-offered cars are usually ones that are tough to sell otherwise.

Autotrader.com

- Owner: Cox Enterprises Inc.
- How it works: By linking with sister company Manheim Auctions, the site has more than 2.2 million used car listings from 40,000 dealers nationwide, searchable by ZIP code or many other ways. Makes money by charging dealers for premium ads.
- The good: It is the biggest car listing service on the Web. If you can't find the car you want here, you don't need one.
- The bad: The vast majority of ads are from dealers, so if you're looking for a cut-rate deal from the little old lady around the corner, you probably won't find it here.

Autobytel.com Inc.

- Owner: Publicly held.
- How it works: Links buyers who are willing to give their names, phone numbers and addresses with a network of 5,000 car dealers nationwide. Makes money from referral fees from dealers.
- The good: With a few clicks, you can shop dozens of dealerships in your area for the exact type of car you're looking for.
- The bad: You have to give up all that personal information. Expect a call from a dealer the next day. Majority of listings are for new cars.

Carsdirect.com Inc.

- Owner: Privately held. Big investors include Amazon.com, Michael Dell and financier George Soros.
- How it works: Like Autobytel, it links buyers to network of 3,000 dealers and gets paid referral fees by dealers. Buyers can also choose to work with a Carsdirect.com "vehicle specialist" who will search dealerships for the specific car you want and arrange a predetermined price.
- The good: Has some of the best car research tools on the Web.
- The bad: With a smaller network of dealers, there's less choice than on other sites. Majority of listings are for new cars.

Go for a Sedan for Teen's First Car, Experts Say

BY AMANDA ROGERS
FORT WORTH STAR-TELEGRAM, NOVEMBER 18, 2003

For most parents, it's a double-edged sword. By the time teens start to drive, they are involved in so many activities that their parents are eager for the day they can drive themselves to school, practice, friends' houses.

On the other hand, there's the fear that their child is entering a phase of life when their actions could lead to serious consequences. According to the Texas Department of Vital Statistics, 498 youngsters between the ages of 15–19 died in motor vehicle accidents in 2001, the leading cause of death for that age group.

Driving, like reading, walking and other important life skills, takes practice, at least a couple of years to become proficient. Even responsible teens who are paying attention will encounter sticky traffic situations that they haven't had practice dealing with. The first time someone slams on the brakes in front of them or their tires skid on a slippery street will be a learning experience.

As one parent says, "It's not if they'll have an accident, it's when. You just pray they'll be all right."

So what's a parent to do? Wrap them up in a couple of tons of steel, advise some local parents in the know.

"I recommend a large, heavy car," says Barbara Jones, driving teacher and co-owner of Right of Way Driving School in Fort Worth.

"When I bought my boys their first cars, I bought them Cadillacs. They're much safer in a big car than they are in a small car, and the insurance was cheaper than it would be on a sport utility vehicle or a sports car."

John Burris, a car salesman at Longhorn Dodge in Fort Worth with 20 years of experience, says most parents are looking for an affordable, dependable car. Safety is also a top priority.

"They want something around their child," Burris says. "They're more concerned about safety, but with today's marketplace they seem to go more with affordability. I wanted some iron around my children. I stuck my two 16-year-olds in SUVs."

AAA Texas has a list of tips for parents seeking a safe car for a teen-ager:

Article by Amanda Rogers from the *Fort Worth Star-Telegram* November 18, 2003. Copyright © *Fort Worth Star-Telegram*. Reprinted with permission.

- Look for a car that handles like the vehicle the teen used when learning to drive, and make sure that it has modern safety features such as airbags and height-adjustable shoulder seatbelts in the front and back seats.

- Go for a sedan, avoiding small, sporty cars, mammoth vehicles and convertibles. Vehicles with a low center of gravity are preferable, instead of top-heavy cars that can turn over.

- Talk to the teen driver about minimizing distractions, such as loud music, cellphones, distracting passengers (especially other teens) and eating while driving.

Insure.com offers a list of the safest vehicles, using crash-test information from the Insurance Institute for Highway Safety and the National Highway Traffic Safety Administration.

Topping the safety charts is a Chrevolet Impala four-door sedan, followed by a Ford Windstar, the Honda Civic four-door, the Lincoln LS, the Toyota Sienna, Volkswagen Jetta four-door, Volkswagen Passat and Volvo S80.

Rates on these vehicles will be lower. Check *www.insure.com* to see how other vehicles did on the crash tests.

Just Taking a Spin

By Jaquetta White
The Times-Picayune (New Orleans), November 4, 2003

When Joyce Smith decided to buy a car a few years ago, she had a pretty good idea of the model she wanted. Not because she had studied different brands in consumer magazines or because she had test-driven them. Smith knew she wanted a Nissan Altima because she had rented it many times when traveling from her Slidell home to Baton Rouge where her daughter was in college.

Although Smith owned three vehicles at the time—she now has four, including the Altima—she found renting a way to avoid adding miles to her own cars and a smart way to test a model she was interested in.

Smith is one of a growing number of drivers who occasionally park their cars and rent vehicles to satisfy a range of needs unrelated to the traditional reason: for transportation from an airport while on a business or leisure trip.

Such drivers tend to rent chic cars to show up in style at a high school reunion or trucks to lug lumber from a store so they won't scratch the roof of the family car. Some, such as Smith, rent practical sedans to test-drive before buying. Others rent cars to avoid putting mileage on their leased vehicles.

"We've gone from one car, one family to multiple cars, one family to multiple cars, one person," said Michael Marsden, a popular culture expert who focuses on automobiles. "We've had almost a monogamous relationship with cars for years. We would buy a car and live in that car for an extended period of time."

Drivers are no longer resigned to the idea that one car must always serve all their purposes, Marsden said.

Rental car companies are noticing this trend.

"If people have a special event such as a class reunion, they will rent a nice car, maybe a Cadillac," said Alexis Hocevar, vice president and general manager of Enterprise Rent-a-Car's south Louisiana group.

White Cadillacs are popular in the spring and summer for people attending weddings, said Alice Pereira, senior public relations associate for Avis Rent-a-Car.

"People like to show up in nice, new, flashy vehicles," she said.

© 2004 The Times-Picayune Publishing Co. All rights reserved. Used with permission of *The Times-Picayune*.

That was Percy Rose's plan in renting a white Cadillac. Though he needed the car for just one day to attend a wedding, he rented it early and used it in the days before and after the ceremony to usher guests to and from the airport.

Excess mileage is a concern that drives many people who lease cars to try renting.

"We wanted to do that in style," said Rose, who owns three cars. "I was able to use it to go and do all my errands."

But renting is not always about image. Smith, the multiple car owner in Slidell, recently rented a car to attend a workshop in Metairie because she didn't want to tack mileage onto one of her own cars.

Excess mileage is a concern that drives many people who lease cars to try renting. Excess mileage on a leased car typically triggers penalties, and some consumers sidestep those penalties by renting a car on occasion.

Renters "have cars at home, but they're leased. They don't want to put the miles on these vehicles," Pereira said.

As more car dealerships push customers to lease, more people may begin to rent, said John MacDonald, vice president of marketing for National and Alamo.

That's why some rental companies have opened more neighborhood locations and lowered rates—some as low as $9.99 a day—to attract frequent renters.

But not all renting is inexpensive and convenient. Some companies charge a base rate of more than $50 a day for luxury cars, sport utility vehicles and minivans, a hefty fee for a renter who already owns a car. And some car rental companies, in an attempt to boost airport business, require that customers rent cars at the airport location if they want to take advantage of special offers.

Hocevar's company, Enterprise, based in St. Louis, commissioned a study of 1,800 drivers and found that about one-third say their own vehicles don't always meet their needs and that one-fourth say they rent for fun and function in the towns where they live.

Avis has started to increase the number of its nonairport locations in response to demand. Enterprise has 21 locations in the New Orleans area. Both of these companies do most of their business from these locations, not the airport.

"It is a trend that we're seeing at Avis. [Renting] is very event-driven," Pereira said.

"Sometimes we have a lot of cars sitting at the airport on the weekend and move them to local locations," Hocevar said.

However, not all companies are leaving the airport to accommodate this group of renters.

"We have a few off-airport locations, but it's not the core of our business," said MacDonald of National and Alamo.

MacDonald said his company has no plans to expand its market to include more off-airport operations.

Since the September 11 attacks, the car rental industry has seen its airport business struggle to rebound. Immediately after the attacks, some companies saw a brief spurt in rentals because some travelers were afraid to fly. For the most part, however, the industry has not been able to recover fully. Revenue for the 10 major car rental companies went from $19.4 billion in 2000 before the attacks to $17.9 billion in 2002, a 7.7 percent decrease, according to Auto Rental News, a car and truck rental trade magazine. Those companies combined have also trimmed their fleets by more than 5 percent to reflect the decrease in demand.

R.I.P. SUVs?

By Peter Roff and Jillian Jonas
United Press International, December 6, 2002

Sport utility vehicles replaced the station wagon in many American families and, like the big wagons before them, are under attack. The recent debate over the question of "What would Jesus drive?" has brought even more attention on the role of SUVs in American life. Calls for increasing the mileage requirements for SUVs have been linked to the suggestion that their owners are giving aid and comfort to Middle Eastern terrorists by keeping the United States dependent on foreign oil. Question: Should SUVs be subjected to a fuel economy regime? UPI political analyst Peter Roff and Jillian Jonas, a freelance journalist living in New York, face off on opposite sides of this critical question.

Jonas: A Scourge on the Public

For those of us not living in Wyoming, SUVs have become a scourge on our cities, to public safety, even to our nation's foreign policy.

They are too big to navigate urban streets, and they have had a deleterious impact on roads and secondary highways which are ill-equipped accommodate the wear and tear they cause.

These gas-guzzlers add to our dependency on foreign oil, a touchy subject as we careen toward war against Iraq. After all, we are the world's biggest consumer of Iraqi oil.

The Bush administration is reviewing a proposal to impose fuel efficiency requirements on SUVs with an eye to killing them according to some critics given the administration's well-documented ties to the auto and oil industries.

Environmental groups maintain these recommendations are actually weaker than what carmakers voluntarily agreed to work toward by 2005. The liberal Sierra Club says 40 mpg by 2012 is already well within reach through existing technology.

The National Academy of Sciences reports carmakers could "raise fuel economy higher . . . than the proposal without compromising safety or making automakers spend more than they can afford."

Copyright 2002 UPI. All rights reserved. This article reprinted with permission. RsiCopyright Clearance License # 3.5981.241439-14946.

The current 20.7 mpg standard was set after the 1973 Arab oil embargo, when light trucks were allowed to get lower efficiency levels than passenger cars because they were primarily used by farmers. Things have changed since then. The soccer mom driving into the city for holiday shopping is not exactly plowing the fields.

As usual, automakers are screaming about the potential costs cutting into huge profits, while also arguing that more fuel efficient SUVs—because of their smaller size—will be less safe than the monsters currently on the roads.

Financially strapped municipalities are being forced to absorb the enormous—and unanticipated—cost of SUVs. Pollution levels in cities are skyrocketing, largely due to huge amounts of corresponding pollutants. Local jurisdictions around Washington recently agreed to a $42 million pollution reduction package to comply with federal clean air standards by the year 2005.

That plan was based on cleaning up 3 tons a day of emissions, well below the new estimates showing levels as high as 47 tons a day in emissions.

Who's going to have to foot the clean-up bills? Not the automakers.

We know from experience that oil imports fall when more fuel-efficient cars are available. Between 1979 and 1985, gasoline use dropped 15 percent and imports plummeted 87 percent. As Dan Becker from the Sierra Club said, "Increasing the fuel economy . . . is the biggest single step the United States can take to reduce our oil dependence and global warming pollution."

Better fuel efficiency on SUVs is just good common sense. It's also the right thing to do.

Roff: **Sputtering, Unwieldy and Vexatious?**

There are many reasons to dislike sport utility vehicles, especially if you're behind one.

Many SUV owners drive them like they were delicate machines, not potential off-road monsters. Think about it: Ever been stuck behind a German-engineered luxury SUV that could get across the Serengeti in a day only to have the driver slow down to two miles an hour to go over a speed bump?

SUVs are easy to hate, making them easy targets for left-leaning environmentalists who don't like development or technology and who don't want people to continue to enjoy the freedom of mobility. The effort to bring SUVs under the CAFE regime is, in reality, merely an attempt to get them off the road.

Soccer moms (and others) love SUVs because they're big. They can tow things. Having an SUV allows little leaguers to carpool. City dwellers may be able to depend on public transportation and singles can get along fine in two-passenger Miatas and Minis; if you have a family of any size you need a big car like an SUV because that is all that is available.

None of that matters to anti-SUV activists. Their mawkish lobbying has gone so far as to make a link to September 11.

"I am ashamed," the Sierra Club's Carl Pope said in March 2002 after Congress turned back their most recent efforts. "I am ashamed that six months after the attack on the World Trade Center the U.S. Senate caved in, not to Osama bin Laden, but to lies from the auto industry." What Pope and others ignore is that many of their complaints stem from the very same standards they successfully lobbied to have placed on an earlier generation of vehicles.

Critics complain that SUVs are hazardous to other vehicles because of their size. Passenger cars are, because of existing the mileage standards, small, light and made of materials that crumple on impact even at low speeds. They are admittedly not equal to SUVs in an accident.

What made passenger cars this way? The existing fuel standards.

The prestigious National Academy of Sciences says 2,600 additional people are killed on the road each year because federal fuel economy standards require the production of cars that are smaller, lighter and, as a direct result, less safe.

Safety is an important consideration—but the data indicates that, to make cars more fuel efficient, they must also be less safe.

The fuel standards also make them more expensive.

The price of new vehicles could increase by as much as $3,000 over the next 10 years if higher mileage requirements are imposed. Higher prices make new cars less affordable, increasing the incentive to keep older, less-fuel efficient, more-polluting vehicles in service longer. In short, the higher standards actually produce the opposite of what proponents say they are intended to do. The demand that the government mandate higher mileage is really about getting SUVs—and people—off the road and keeping them off.

Drivers Stick with Light Trucks Despite Heavy Fuel Prices

By Gregory Cancelada
St. Louis Post-Dispatch, May 30, 2004

Though many drivers are grousing about high prices at the gasoline pump, analysts and economists don't expect the spike in oil prices to trigger an exodus from light trucks to more fuel-efficient passenger vehicles.

Unless prices continue to rise and stay above today's levels for an extended period, consumers will continue to buy light trucks—which include pickups, sport utility vehicles, minivans and vans—because of space and other features not found in passenger vehicles, analysts say.

Even if gasoline prices stayed well above $2 per gallon for the rest of the summer, "I would argue that it will make them choose among the more fuel-efficient SUVs and light trucks," said Robert Schnorbus, chief economist at J. D. Power and Associates. "It won't get them to switch out of trucks into smaller cars."

Analysts also say the effects of higher oil prices on auto demand will be muted because there are key differences between today's price run-up and big price shocks triggered by the Arab oil embargo in 1973 and the Shah of Iran's overthrow in 1979.

The auto industry doesn't doubt that the recent rise in oil prices is causing people to take a closer look at fuel efficiency when buying a car.

U.S. regular unleaded gasoline averaged $2.06 for the week ended May 24, a record level that was up 39 percent from the same period a year ago.

But analysts don't see a general shift in consumer purchasing.

If oil prices stop climbing, there isn't too much risk of a large shift in consumer demand to vehicles with greater fuel efficiency, said Valerie A. Ramey, a professor of economics at the University of California at San Diego.

"The reason is gasoline prices are still much lower in real terms than they were in 1981," she said.

To be the equivalent in 1981 prices, today's gasoline prices would have to be roughly $3.10 a gallon, said Ramey, who has studied the impact of oil prices on the U.S. auto industry.

"It's just not as dramatic yet," she said. "Now, if it continues, you might see people shifting."

Reprinted with permission of the *St. Louis Post-Dispatch*, copyright 2004.

At the same time, a key question is whether gasoline prices are sustainable, said George Pipas, U.S. sales analysis manager at Ford Motor Co.

"Will they go up to $2.50 and stay there for the next six to seven months? Then, I think you might see something manifest itself. But as yet, it is hardly discernible at all," Pipas said.

Weaker Sales

Poorer-than-expected auto sales last month triggered a rush of stories that gas-guzzlers were on their way out.

All light-vehicle sales were up only 0.6 percent last month, but April's sales of large SUVs—such as the Ford Expedition, Chevrolet Suburban and Toyota Sequoia—were down 15 percent versus a year ago, according to J. D. Power and Associates.

Sustained high oil prices might end up hurting midsized SUVs . . . rather than large SUVs as consumers move to smaller SUVs.

But analysts say the dip in sales is more likely due to aggressive incentives last year for large SUVs rather than a shift away from these vehicles. Plus, overall vehicle demand was disappointing in April.

Meanwhile, light-truck demand continued to grow faster than demand for cars last month. Light-truck sales were up 2.7 percent in April, and those for passenger cars were down 1.7 percent, J. D. Power says.

Disappointing sales in April and growing vehicle inventories might be due more to the events in Iraq and the stumbling stock market, Schnorbus said. "It's possible that consumers are getting a little cautious."

Schnorbus said sales are likely to improve over the summer as automakers clear out their inventories.

"If that doesn't happen and if it's not happening at the gas-guzzling end of the market, then we'll start having a basis for concluding that energy prices really are having a major impact."

Sustained high oil prices might end up hurting midsized SUVs—like the Ford Explorer—rather than large SUVs as consumers move to smaller SUVs such as the RAV4 of Toyota Motor Corp., said Dave Lucas, vice president of Autodata Corp., which tracks sales.

"A lot of the people in the large SUV segment need those vehicles for a reason."

The domestic auto industry has good reason to be nervous with rising fuel prices. General Motors Corp., Ford Motor Co. and the Chrysler Group of DaimlerChrysler AG were hit hard when consumers fled from gas-guzzlers to smaller, fuel-efficient Japanese imports in the 1970s and early 1980s.

"Big increases in oil prices can wreak absolute havoc in the auto industry," Ramey said, pointing to the massive restructuring that automakers underwent.

In the aftermath of the 1973 oil embargo, they were forced to shut down plants and convert them to make smaller cars, she said.

Even then, the automakers were left with excessive production capacity, she said. "Consumers wanted a different kind of car than [what] the U.S. automakers could make."

Though the traditional Big Three learned to build cars with better gas mileage, they also moved aggressively into light trucks such as minivans and SUVs when oil prices abated in the 1980s.

Light trucks accounted for nearly two-thirds of their light-vehicle sales last year, so a sudden switch in consumer demand for these vehicles would be devastating.

At the same time, a shift out of light trucks would have a direct impact on the St. Louis economy as local plants make this type of vehicle: DaimlerChrysler, whose two plants assemble pickups and minivans in Fenton; Ford, which builds sport utility vehicles in Hazelwood; and GM, which makes full-size vans in Wentzville.

"If there were a big shift, you could expect some of these factories to be converted back to small cars," she said.

No Rerun

Still, analysts don't expect a rerun of 1973 or 1979.

When oil prices began to rise in 1973, there had been a lot of talk about dwindling oil reserves and speculation that higher prices would be permanent. After the second shock started in 1979, consumers became convinced that the rising price of oil was the new reality, Ramey said.

Since the collapse of oil prices in 1986, price increases have been less permanent, she said. "You'll see these temporary run-ups, and then you'll see them run down, so I think people are less likely at this point to think these prices must be permanent."

"People sort of got their blinders on when they're looking at fuel prices and not the total economic picture."— George Pipas, Ford Motor Co.

The oil shocks also created periods when gasoline was rationed rather than sold at a market-clearing price, she said. "That is the kind of thing that will really make people switch."

But the two earlier price run-ups occurred during tough economic times. Today's increase in fuel prices is occurring when the economy shows strong growth, jobs are being added at an increasing pace and interest rates are near historic lows, Pipas said.

"I think what is muting the impact of higher fuel prices is that almost all the other economic fundamentals are about as good a script that one could write," he said. "People sort of got their blinders on when they're looking at fuel prices and not the total economic picture."

Still, Ramey believes the domestic automakers should hedge their bets and invest more in hybrid electric vehicles, which use an electric motor in addition to a diesel or gasoline engine. The electric motor is powered by batteries that charge when the vehicle is braking or idling.

"If I were a manager at one of the auto companies, I would get those engineers to make sure they had some good plans for hybrid cars," she said.

If gasoline prices stay at today's levels, there could be a gradual shift to hybrids, particularly among lower-income consumers more sensitive to gasoline prices, Ramey said.

Toyota and Honda sell hybrid passenger cars that offer high levels of fuel efficiency. The Toyota Prius gets about 56 miles a gallon, combined highway and city, and the Honda Civic gets about 48 miles a gallon.

Consumers will get a wider choice this year when automakers start offering hybrid pickups and SUVs. Among the vehicles will be a Ford Escape SUV, built in Claycomo, Mo., that will get about 36 miles per gallon.

Schnorbus isn't so sure that large numbers of consumers will flock to hybrids.

Gasoline prices are extremely high in Europe, but there isn't big demand for hybrids in that market, he said.

Retail premium gasoline prices for the week of May 17 averaged $5.46 per gallon the United Kingdom, $5.38 in Germany and $5.05 in France. They averaged $2.19 in the United States, according to the Energy Department.

II. Marketing and Design

Editors' Introduction

The goal, of course, behind automotive marketing and design is to compel consumers to purchase a particular vehicle. Automakers target ads to specific types of people, secure celebrity endorsements, hire "car shrinks" to plumb the human subconscious for signs as to what people want to drive, and even improve the vehicles themselves. In a world where our wants are somewhat schizophrenic—Safe but cheap! Massive but fuel-efficient! Reliable but cool!—car makers maintain a frenzied pace to churn out vehicles that they think consumers will find attractive.

Vicki Haddock explains in "Car-nal Knowledge" that one reason why drivers so badly want the perfect auto is because, since their inception, cars have steadily become intertwined with an individual's sense of self. Vehicles are no longer mere status symbols (and certainly not just means of conveyance), but now reflect how drivers want to be perceived by their fellow motorists. "The old axiom 'you are what you drive' has been firmly supplanted by something more exacting: 'You drive what you want people to think you are,'" Haddock professes.

Evidently, the images drivers wish to convey change frequently, as industry executives lament that they must continuously struggle to keep up with consumer demand for fresh, novel vehicles. In "Survival Demands Automakers Race to Bring New Models to Market Faster," Bill Vlasic explains that, in trying to match the speed of Japanese plants, domestic car companies have reduced the concept-to-production time to under two years, and they are pushing for even faster results. Cars now have an average "showroom age" of 2.2 years, or half of what it was in the early 1990s. Such frenzied efforts are expensive and anxiety-inducing, and mistakes are costly. Nevertheless, domestic automakers seem resigned to maintain the pace.

One discovery that carmakers have made is that, post-September 11, many drivers have focused more on the safety of their autos. William Diem elaborates upon this concept in "Global Mood Affects Vehicle Design," explaining that, at the moment, many drivers do not seem to care as much about how splashy or elegant their cars are as long as they are safe and, if possible, look a bit like tanks. The massive, boxy Hummer is a perfect example of this sort of thinking. However, some have taken a different lesson from the terror attacks and turned in the opposite direction, preferring small, fuel-efficient cars that do not necessitate a reliance on imported oil. One such vehicle is the Smart car, a tiny, inexpensive, environmentally friendly auto that averages 60 miles per hour and can squeeze into miniscule parking spaces. In the past, Smart cars have been two-seaters, but in January 2004 Smart began production on its first four-seater. Although Smart vehicles are currently only available in Europe, Anthony Lewis announces in "Smart Lesson in Quality" that the new Smart SUV is scheduled to make its debut in the United States in 2006.

Whether a vehicle is compact and eco-friendly, spacious and sporty, or glamorous and sleek, automakers need to properly market their products to consumers, and one of the most sought-after groups of consumers is Generation Y, loosely defined as children born between approximately 1980 and 1995. Though they currently account for only five percent of new car sales, the 63 million members of Gen Y will buy 25 percent by 2010 and 40 percent by 2020, so car makers are intent on wooing them before they reach the apex of their buying power. One of the problems that Matt Nauman illustrates in "Car Makers Zooming in on Youth" is that Gen Y buyers do not like to be marketed to or told what to buy. Toyota, for example, is trying to shed its somewhat fusty, Baby Boomer image with the advent of the Scion, a car targeted to Gen Y-ers in that it is "smaller, cheaper, faster and—with a lot of speakers—louder." Essentially, teenagers and adults in their early 20s want cars that are inexpensive but still carry a cool cachet.

Less important to Generation Y, but increasingly coveted by older drivers, are in-car information services and tracking systems. These so-called telematics rely on global positioning systems (GPS) to guide drivers with maps and directions, and to summon help in emergency situations. However, the growing popularity of telematics has sparked a debate about what other services they should provide. Some systems mention "points of interest," or nearby gas stations, pharmacies, restaurants, etc. T. Edward Phillips provides a survey of such systems in his article "Lost? Let the Car Be Your Guide." Although GPS has only recently become standard in many newer luxury vehicles, Philips explains that older cars can also be fitted fairly easily with these so-called aftermarket systems.

Car-nal Knowledge

By Vicki Haddock
San Francisco Chronicle, July 13, 2003

The old axiom "you are what you drive" has been firmly supplanted by something more exacting: "You drive what you want people to think you are."

Automakers, who have long sold cars as status symbols, are today reaching unprecedented levels of scientific precision and cynical sophistication: they've hired psychologists, psychiatrists and anthropologists to help market cars to our deepest emotional desires.

It's been a lot of miles on the road since that summer 100 years ago when Ford Motor Co. incorporated and then began marketing its Model T's. Even a visionary like Henry Ford could scarcely have imagined the proliferation of today's makes and models—the 26 million registered vehicles in California now outnumber licensed drivers by 6 million—nor how a hunk of metal could become so intertwined in Americans' sense of ourselves.

And he certainly couldn't have foreseen "car shrinks"—men like Clothaire Rapaille of Palm Beach, whose Jungian archetypal research for Daimler-Chrysler had test consumers lying on mats in low light and free-associating to music. The goal: to concoct a new small car that would bypass their brains' logical cortex and hit their "reptilian hot buttons."

"People said, 'It's a jungle out there. It's Mad Max. People want to kill me, rape me.'"

Rapaille expounds. "The message to designers was clear. 'Give me a big thing like a tank'"—even if it was a small model. The test group also craved something that could distinguish them from every other look-alike on the road.

The result: the retro-hip PT Cruiser.

That research would influence the development and marketing of other vehicles, including the poseur Hummer H2. A Hummer pre-emptively shouts, "I'm overpowering!"—unless, of course, it's yellow, which undercuts the machismo with the message "Umm, just kidding!"

Suddenly, "emotion" is the big word in Motown, as in 'we want vehicles that make an emotional connection,'" *Fortune* Magazine has noted. "It's as if the industry had relocated en masse to Marin County."

Republished with permission of *The San Francisco Chronicle*, from "Car-nal Knowledge," by Vicki Haddock, July 13, 2003; permission conveyed through Copyright Clearance Center, Inc.

Some 50 years ago, when sociologist Vance Packard wrote his expose, *The Hidden Persuaders,* about the psycho-probers of the ad world, the country was appalled. Packard predicted that eventually "all this depth manipulation of the psychological variety will seem amusingly old-fashioned."

He was right—not, as he hoped, because exposure made it taboo, but because success made it seemingly indispensable.

Today's consultants have sliced and diced the vehicle-buying public into as many as 62 different demographic and lifestyle microcosms—with names such as "Blue Blood Estates," "New Ecotopia," "Young Literati," and "Shotguns and Pickups."

Automakers hire hypnotists, dream analysts and a host of other spelunkers of the subconscious, sporting either brilliant mind theory or ebullient psychobabble.

They then refine prototypes and aim ads directly at your psychographic profile, your "emotional pulse"—the rather irrational factor that make some vehicles particularly comely in your eyes.

Consultants have sliced and diced the vehicle-buying public into as many as 62 different demographic and lifestyle microcosms.

How else to persuade you to do the inherently irrational: shell out thousands of dollars for an item that loses about a quarter of its value the instant you drive it off the lot?

"Forget focus groups. What we've done is come up with approaches that really get into your souls," says Chris Cedergren, whose Southern California-based firm, Iceology, has clinical psychologists on staff and has consulted for most major automakers. People tell focus groups they want an SUV for its usefulness, safety, carpool convenience and cargo capacity.

As Henry Ford might say—Bunk! Based on those criteria, they should have bought a minivan.

"Most people who drive an SUV never actually take it off-road," Cedergren notes. "These vehicles became cool because they connote all the values that people want to be: aggressive, sitting high, muscular, full of action and adventure—with the freedom to go wherever they want whenever they want.

"Typically, you really want a vehicle to be about sex. You want to say (driving this car) is the same ecstasy as sex."

Of course, some cars do more obvious peacock-strutting than others. Juliet MacCannell, professor emerita of comparative literature at UC Irvine, has observed the symbolic contradiction of "going topless" in a convertible—human exposure and vulnerability sitting astride cold, hard machinery.

Auto analysts are more crass, privately referring to sports and muscle cars as "vehicle viagra."

An episode of *Friends* illustrates the perils of perception: On turning 30, Ross splurges on an MGB, prompting Chandler to ask, "Wouldn't it have been cheaper to just stuff a sock down there?" Ross insists, "That's not what this is about. I . . . I am a sports car enthusiast. I have always been into cars." When Joey asks about the horsepower, though, Ross giddily shrugs: "I don't know, but look how shiny . . ."

Then a fat, bald guy pulls alongside in the identical car and exults, "How hot are we!"—instantly prompting Ross to sell it.

Pop culture notwithstanding, demographic data can be eerily precise. The Prizm marketing database, for example, concluded that the microcosm of consumers likely to have a second mortgage, buy wine by the case, eat natural cold cereal and read Architectural Digest was more likely to buy BMW 5-series cars. Conversely, they are unlikely to hunt, eat canned stews, watch *Wheel of Fortune* or buy Chevys.

It isn't just analysts who label vehicle owners—fellow citizens do, too. You can take an online quiz to peg your personality courtesy of Charles Kenny, who heads the Memphis consumer psychology firm Kenny & Associates.

For example, he concludes, a gold PT Turbo says you see the best times behind you. A silver BMW says you want a little notice but mostly desire a pleasurable driving experience. A red Ford Mustang Mach 1 says you're in it for the fun. A black Saturn sedan says you want to be cared for.

Driving a blue Toyota Camry tells the world you're reliable, dependable, but perhaps slightly boring—which explains why Toyota is running ads depicting a speeding driver doing a 180-degree-turn on the freeway in a Camry.

When a multinational ad agency hired University of Florida professor of English and advertising James Twitchell as a consultant, it was trying to convince its client, Volvo, that an upscale version of the sensible Swedish sedan could be rebranded as a luxury item. The goal: to move it to where the profits are, from entree to dessert.

"My job, for which I was paid the equivalent of teaching many, many hours of Wordsworth, was to help the agency staff think about how to do it—not how to compose the ad but how to convince Ford (which had acquired Volvo) that language and image could make Volvo sumptuous, Twitchell writes, in *Living It Up—America's Love Affair with Luxury.*

"What I thought was interesting is that the agency people never seemed to question their ability to transform this pumpernickel of a car into a brioche."

Peculiar Reasons

Of course, however much the marketing mavens relish sorting us into categories, the reasons we purchase vehicles are peculiar and complex.

You, for example, may insist that you buy a car simply to get from point A to point B. Perhaps you're destined to buy a Honda Civic or Toyota Corolla—cars marketed to buyers who take pride in being practical and no-nonsense.

"I drive a Toyota Corolla now, and like to think that's a car that makes no statement," says Robert Thompson, professor of media and popular culture at Syracuse University. "But the truth is that I, too, am playing the game, driving a message.

"As a cynical, intellectual type, I'm telling people I'm immune to playing the consumer game. When I pull into the faculty parking lot with the other fancy cars, I congratulate myself for what I drive. In fact, my windshield cracked mysteriously six months ago and I haven't fixed it yet, which only furthers my sense of reverse snobbery."

Clearly money isn't the sole factor in car-buying.

When he was the richest man in the United States, Sam Walton explained why he continued to drive his old pickup: "What am I supposed to haul my dogs around in, a Rolls-Royce?"

The pickup telegraphed a salient message to Wal-Mart customers—Walton was a no-frills guy who knew how to save a buck.

Cameron Diaz's Statement

When Cameron Diaz bought a hybrid Toyota Prius, her statement wasn't "I'm a rich party girl;" rather, "I'm socially responsible and probably care more about the environment than you."

Once upon a time, Cadillac held unparalleled cachet as a classy car, but it fell victim to the Boomers' fierce rebellion against their parents' tastes and values. For several years, the stereotype was that the only drivers under 70 who'd be caught dead in a Caddy were pimps; the brand developed rigor mortis.

Today, struggling not to follow the Lincoln Town Car into the graveyard, Cadillac unveiled its CTS in ads featuring Led Zeppelin's "Been a long time since I rock and rolled . . .," and its vehicles are featured in *The Matrix Reloaded*, and hip-hop music videos. The goal, as Cadillac general manager Mark LaNeve put it: "to make Cadillac cool again."

Honda Buyers Aging

Honda, whose buyer base is aging into their 40s and 50s, is trying to avert the same fate with its new Element, aimed at active Generation Y drivers who want to be transported to spots to surf, kayak and mountain bike in an affordable vehicle that can carry cumbersome gear, give them a place to sleep on the road and be hosed out. (Early returns suggest the vehicle is more popular with older Boomers.)

The Xterra focuses on a similar buyer. Jerry Hirschberg, president of Nissan Design International, told Auto World he really wanted to introduce the vehicle "pre-scuffed," like stone-washed jeans. Alas, the sales department balked.

"The auto industry is very similar to the fashion industry" said consultant Cedergren. "A car is like a garment, and nowhere do people wear their cars more than California, where you can't get anywhere driving on jammed freeways, anyway."

Retro cars are case studies in emotional response. There's the Volkswagen Beetle, which analysts say Boomers embraced to rekindle the past, soothe modern stresses and publicly endorse the anti-materialism mantra of the 1960s while simultaneously relishing creature comforts. The Ford Thunderbird returned, evoking lost youth. And the PT Cruiser drew Gen X and Y buyers, who exhibit a surprising fascination with cultural history.

This year's fad car is the Mini Cooper. Although buyers come from a demographic cross-section, analysts say most people who purchase this petite eye-catcher are strivers sharing some common needs: to attract attention and project "trendy."

"A car is an identity you carry with you even outside your home," said Thompson. "If you read old cowboy memoirs and literature, the relationship you had with your horse was a really strong one. You spent a lot of time on your horse, you cared for it, cowboys sang songs about them. Feeling really good about your horse was really important."

Of course, every region of the country carries its own preferences, which explains why Saab, with its relatively small penetration in the American market, does robust business in the Bay Area. Drivers here tend to see themselves as cosmopolitan and sophisticated—suffice it to say that for many of them, tooling around in a Buick is the automotive equivalent of broadcasting, "I'm bourgeois!"

"This is why we think it's critical to use psychologists," insists Cedergren. "Even the most intelligent consumers will base expensive purchases on the most trivial details—like one person saying you look about 10 years younger test driving that car. Boom! That one statement made the sale."

But car buyers who opt to make a statement at the top of their lungs risk the ricochets of ridicule.

Some may call Hummer owners paramilitary porkers. They may joke that a convertible buyer has gotten himself a "substitute mistress." And they may guilt-trip gas-guzzling SUV drivers, pointing out the ozone hole opening up over them.

"We almost can't help ourselves from judging people by what they drive, which makes us all easy fodder for the automobile industry," says media professor Thompson.

"It's the same with a car. Buying a car is like a New Year's resolution, it's like the minute after you take communion, it's springtime, it's rebirth, it's the chance to temporarily reinvent yourself to be whatever you want to be.

"And it comes complete with a 'new' smell."

Survival Demands Automakers Race to Bring New Models to Market Faster

BY BILL VLASIC
THE DETROIT NEWS, JANUARY 5, 2004

Assembly plants hustle to shave minutes off the time to build a car. Product cycles shrink in a mad dash to bring new models to market. The window of opportunity for a new-vehicle launch seems as short as the opening of a Hollywood movie.

The global automotive industry is moving at unprecedented speed, flooding showrooms with all-new cars and trucks in a frenetic race to capture the hearts of fickle consumers.

With a glut of worldwide capacity, automakers from Detroit to Munich to Tokyo are consumed with streamlining operations, executing faster and beating rivals to new segments. It is a race to survive.

The new rules of the road are crystal clear: Throttle up—or get left behind in the fast lane of the 21st century American auto market.

"What may have been fast enough in the past is no longer good enough today," said General Motors Corp. Vice Chairman Bob Lutz.

Once considered dinosaurs of heavy industry stuck in a Rust Belt mentality, Detroit's Big Three automakers are sprinting to keep pace with nimbler competitors from Japan and South Korea.

No more 48-month product programs, laborious launches or endless rounds of market research. In today's get-it-now culture of immediate gratification, the luxury of time is a quaint memory.

"The issue of speed is critical to us because our customer changes their mind a lot," said Jim Farley, head of Toyota Motor Corp.'s youth-driven Scion brand.

"Four-year cycles just won't cut it."

It's no contest for the faint of heart.

Ford Motor Co. and DaimlerChrysler AG's Chrysler Group have stumbled with sluggish product plans that trail the rapid-fire output of Toyota, Honda Motor Co. and Nissan Motor Co.

GM, the most efficient domestic manufacturer, can't match the assembly time of the best Japanese plants operating in North America.

The margin for error on a product debut is weeks, not months. If a new car or truck doesn't hit the mark fast, chances are it will fade from consumers' consciousness even faster.

Reprinted with permission from *The Detroit News*.

Cost of Speed

Every aspect of the industry has shifted into a higher gear—design, engineering, supplier input, manufacturing, advertising and marketing.

But with speed comes the danger of uneven quality, rushed decisions and "me-too" products that require costly incentives to prop up sales.

Over the next three years, automakers will introduce an average of 57 new models annually, a 70 percent increase over the norm recorded since 1991, according to Merrill Lynch auto analyst John Casesa.

"This trend is, of course, fabulous for consumers, but expensive for producers who must maintain fresh product lines despite shrinking profit margins," Casesa said.

By 2006, the average "showroom age" of vehicles on sale will be 2.2 years—half what it was in the early 1990s. Moreover, an astounding 82 percent of the industry's U.S. volume will be replaced with new product over the next three years.

"Everybody is trying to bring vehicles out more quickly," said Jed Connelly, Nissan's North American sales chief. "Concept-to-production time is down to less than two years, and people have talked about going to less than a year."

After trailing the Japanese for years, Detroit's automakers have revved up their new-product machinery.

GM will replace a quarter of its volume in the 2005 model year and nearly 35 percent the year after. Ford is also hitting the accelerator, replacing more than half of its product line in the next 24 months, according to Merrill Lynch.

With speed comes the danger of uneven quality, rushed decisions and "me-too" products that require costly incentives to prop up sales.

"Detroit is back on the offensive," Casesa said.

But with Asian automakers adding new factory capacity in the United States, the competition will only intensify. Nissan's new assembly plant in Mississippi opened last year and already is poised to launch its fourth light-truck product.

The newer the product, the less need there is to pile on costly rebates and lease deals to move the metal. But the penalty for botching a marketing launch is severe.

Chrysler rolled out its Pacifica crossover wagon last year to great fanfare. Supported by a huge ad campaign featuring singer Celine Dion, the Pacifica launch was a critical step in the strategy to take the Chrysler brand upscale.

But the moody Dion television spots fell flat, and consumers blanched at the $40,000 sticker prices on the first shipments of fully loaded Pacificas. In a few short weeks, Pacifica lost its luster as Chrysler scrambled to relaunch it with lower prices and more generic ads.

The lesson? Get the launch right immediately, or pay the price.

Taking a Gamble

In the rush to fill niches in the marketplace, automakers increasingly roll the dice on edgy concepts and designs adapted from existing vehicle platforms.

Sometimes the tactic yields surprise hits, such as the funky Honda Element sport utility. But just as often it leads to spectacular mistakes like GM's bizarre Pontiac Aztek SUV.

The proliferation of product is taking brands in directions that test their limits. Prime examples include Chrysler's upcoming upscale rear-wheel-drive sedans, Volkswagen AG's Phaeton luxury sedan, Porsche AG's first sport ute and BMW's little 1-series compact line.

"These companies are taking enormous gambles in new segments," said Joseph Phillippi of the consulting firm Auto Trends in Short Hills, N.J.

Above all, getting quicker means getting leaner, and that costs jobs on the factory floor. GM, Ford and Chrysler won much-needed concessions in their latest United Auto Workers contract for job reductions to narrow the productivity gap with Japanese plants.

Slashing personnel only goes so far. The key to matching Toyota or Nissan lies in flexible manufacturing equipment and work rules that quicken the process of building cars and their components.

GM improved its U.S. plant productivity 6.4 percent last year, according to the 2003 edition of the Harbour Report that calculates the average number of worker-hours needed to assemble a vehicle.

The improvements cut GM's average assembly time to 24 hours per vehicle, still three hours more than Toyota needs to build a car in its U.S. plants.

"GM has gotten a lot faster, but what exactly did they catch up to?" asked Ron Harbour, president of Harbour and Associates of Troy. "Are they just catching up to where Toyota was two or three years ago?"

But even incremental improvements in assembly time pay off on the bottom line. Harbour noted that GM earned an average profit of $701 per vehicle in 2002, compared with $337 the previous year.

"There's no secret to getting faster," Harbour said. "You design vehicles for easier assembly, improve quality to eliminate repairs at the end of the line, and, above all, reduce overtime."

Building cars faster not only improves earnings, but also allows the manufacturer to stay closer to its customers. Nissan cranked out a raft of new models over the past three years. Now it is paring the time to fill dealer lots with the most popular option packages and vehicle colors.

"We are speeding up the order cycle," Connelly said. "Within six days prior to production, we can change the orders in the bank to reflect the market."

Impatient Customers

In a world of built-to-order computers and Internet shopping, consumers are showing less patience for the car-buying experience. Younger customers, in particular, are in a hurry to get what they want.

Toyota's Scion brand offers just two models, and the division employs a strict no-haggle pricing strategy. But even with transaction times averaging fewer than three hours, the younger generation wants to get in and out of the showroom in a hurry.

"The under-25-year-olds are the most critical people in terms of timeliness," Farley said. "I don't think we knew just how demanding this generation of customers is."

Executives at Detroit's Big Three automakers cringe at the admiring media accounts of the efficiency and speed of their Japanese rivals—and they are determined to change the perception.

As proof of its streamlined product process, Ford points to the Shelby Cobra concept car unveiled at the 2004 North American International Auto Show in Detroit.

> *In a world of built-to-order computers and Internet shopping, consumers are showing less patience for the car-buying experience.*

"We did it in less than nine months, which is very, very fast," said Ford design head J Mays. "We had something to prove not only to ourselves, but also to the financial community."

There may be no better example of the need for speed than the Pontiac Solstice, a two-seat roadster that GM first showed as a concept two years ago. At this year's show—just 24 months later— GM is ready to put Solstice into production.

By designing a concept that needed few changes for production, GM cut months from the process of bringing Solstice to the U.S. market.

"This is a 24-month program, and we were running at 48 months just five years ago," said Mark Hogan, head of GM's advanced vehicle development. "Roadsters have a shorter shelf life, and we had to go as fast as possible."

Hogan calls the Solstice, which is built on GM's versatile new Kappa rear-wheel-drive platform, a "breakthrough effort" in GM's accelerated development process.

A breakthrough effort, but hardly acceptable in the long run.

"We have competitors who are doing major face-lifts on models in 12 months' time," Hogan said. "I don't know if there's any end-game."

Speed. It's no longer just a measure of horsepower and zero-to-60 times on the test track. Every aspect of the industry is now judged on the clock.

The industry's basic business model may not be changing, but the game has gotten faster and less forgiving.

Get to market early with a hit, and the rewards can be awesome. But lag, and the consequences are painful. In the auto industry of today, there's the quick—and the walking wounded.

Global Mood Affects Vehicle Design

By William Diem
Detroit Free Press, March 19, 2003

War, the threat of war and economic uncertainty have less effect on future cars than on future fashion, but together they may be nudging the industry away from extravagance.

Patrick LeQument, the senior vice president of design at Renault SA, said the difficult times push car designers to "a return toward sure values and rejection of superficial things. Customers have a need for safety and authenticity; they reject the flamboyant and extreme." LeQument was one of several designers attending this month's Geneva auto show who spoke about the link among unsettled times, fashion and automobile design.

Renault introduced the successor to its Scenic family minivan at the Geneva show, as well as a convertible with a solid glass and steel roof and anti-submarining air bags in the front seats.

Michael Mauer, who heads design at Saab in Sweden, said the trend toward SUVs in the United States is the auto industry's reaction to "an expression of a kind of need or wish for people to protect themselves, to have a safe shell around them," and Saab is considering such a vehicle.

Much of the clothing shown recently for fall is heavily influenced by thoughts of war. Sean (P. Diddy) Combs told the *New York Times* that his line of jumpsuits, padded pants and leather motocross jackets were warrior clothes. Calvin Klein put military corners at the shoulders, and Nicole Miller used fabrics the color of army fatigues.

In the auto industry, said Mauer, "the decision for future portfolios has to be done a little more carefully. Smart had the experience of trying to do a car that was launched like a watch, and then they found out it was not just 100 euros, it was 10,000 euros. If you pay 10,000 euros you think twice how fashionable your product should be."

Smart is the tiny two-seater from DaimlerChrysler AG that began as a joint venture between Swiss watch company Swatch AG and Mercedes-Benz.

Article by William Diem from the *Detroit Free Press* March 19, 2003. Copyright © *Detroit Free Press*. Reprinted with permission.

Martin Ehlarik, senior interior designer for Nissan Europe, believes society is pushing the industry toward more responsible vehicles. "People are more introspective," he said, "and designers should offer more responsible products.

When I saw the cars in Detroit (at the North American International Auto Show in January) with all the mega engines, and there is the potential of war, I thought it was being a bit irresponsible.

"The industry goes in cycles of extravagance, then backs off. Now we have all these cars like the Maybach, the Bugatti Veyron, the new Rolls-Royce. I think we're going to see another cycle where these sorts of products take a back seat for 10 or 12 years."

Some designers said that they were not affected by the current climate, or that the effects were not obvious.

"We need to keep the product cycles going and develop cars that will last," said Moray Callum, a former Ford designer assigned to lead Mazda's design department 18 months ago. "Fuel economy may

---

Martin Ehlarik, senior interior designer for Nissan Europe, believes society is pushing the industry toward more responsible vehicles.

---

suddenly become more fashionable if war were to break out, God forbid, and it may result in a relook at cycle times and what kind of vehicles will be developed in the future, but long term, we're not going to stop designing cars."

At Volvo, brand values are already lined up with society's concern for safety. "Maybe people will be looking at safer cars," said Pr Heyden, who designed the interior of Volvo's Versatility concept car after starting his career at Volvo three years ago. He noted that the XC90 sport utility, which Volvo bills as the safest sport-utility, has "sold more than we expected."

Design at BMW AG is unaffected, said chief designer Chris Bangle, an American.

"We talk about it and we get on to business," he said. "At BMW, we have a positive outlook on the world economic situation. We design cars for customers who are successful."

BMW showed bullet-proof versions of its 3-and 7-series cars at the Geneva show, but they look the same on the outside as normal cars.

Although Saab is considering a car for people who "like to sit high, to have this overview, to have this protection feeling," said Mauer. "I don't know if terror or war will lead to even more cars like this. In the U.S. some people say if you buy an SUV you support the terror because you support the oil industry with the fuel consumption. Maybe that could lead to a totally opposite direction, that people are more aware of this and start to drive Smarts, even in the U.S."

Smart Lesson in Quality

By Anthony Lewis
Automotive Industries, March 2004

Sitting in the cantina in downtown Smartville, you look down on all your failures as you eat lunch. The top-floor restaurant, along with the French factory's administrative offices, overlook the re-work station, the centerpiece of the cross-shaped Smart Car plant.

As they eat, workers from the automaker and suppliers alike can chew over how much bonus they will lose if the re-work station is too full.

It's a concept, along with many, many more which could soon be finding its way across the North Atlantic. Plant managers from across DaimlerChrysler in general and Jeep in particular, are regular visitors to Smartville—so called because the plant comprises 14 buildings and is shared with six systems suppliers: Magna Chassis & Uniport, Surtemal/Eisenmann, Siemens VDO, Dynamit Nobel, Cubic Europe and Thyssen Krupp.

The production concepts in Hambach, in the Lorraine region of France, just two hours drive from DaimlerChrysler HQ in Stuttgart, Germany, will also be making their way across the South Atlantic.

A new Smart SUV, to be called the "formore," and due for hunch in the United States in 2006, is to be built at the DCX plant at Juiz de Fora, in Brazil.

This factory currently produces the Mercedes-Benz A-class but will become the center of worldwide production for the SUV.

According to Helmut Wawra, Smart's head of design and engineering, most suppliers for the project will be European.

"Because of the size of our engineering department, it is important suppliers have the ability to carry out engineering work close to us in Germany and have plants in Brazil, this is the case certainly for the Tier 1 suppliers."

The United States will be the main market for the Smart SUV taking 50 percent of production. Wawra says: "It will obviously be a very important car for our brand because it will be the first Smart car in that market. With the federal regulations involved, we will not be introducing any other Smart products there until the next generation City Smart (now called fortwo)."

Article by Anthony Lewis from *Automotive Industries* March 2004. Copyright © *Automotive Industries*. Reprinted with permission.

Slingshot Salvo

The United has already had a glimpse of what Smart can do. The Chrysler Slingshot concept on stand at the Detroit auto show in January is based on the Smart Roadster platform—but it will not make it to market.

Smart Design and Engineering Chief Helmut Wawra said: "The Slingshot was a very exciting concept, but it does not meet Federal requirements. What it does is show how Smart can fit into the DaimlerChrysler group in terms of research and new model development across all the brands.

"Slingshot is a great idea, a sports car with the fuel consumption of our City Coupe. The idea was to show the United States government what is possible in terms of reducing fuel consumption without having to invest in expensive hybrids."

Does Wawra think diesel can make it in the United States? "There has to be a change in perception," he says. The diesel engine is still perceived as dirty, smelly, noisy and slow. They are big barriers to overcome. But sales of Mercedes-Benz and Volkswagen diesels are growing in North America and we expect the passenger car market to grow slowly.

"The advantage of a diesel over hybrids is that it is a know quantity. There is still a lot of development work to be done on hybrids and the technology is changing and evolving all the time. Diesel has a proven track record and is reliable."

Between now and launch at the Detroit Auto Show in 2006 there are a lot of tests to be passed to meet ES Federal regulations. "Emissions tests are particularly time consuming and it is a challenge to squeeze it all in to the time schedule," added Wawra.

He said that Smart would not have its own retail chain in North America but will almost certainly use the Mercedes-Benz network. "Our colleagues at Mercedes-Benz have a lot of experience in the North American market from things such as Federal regulations to the special expectations of the consumers in the united States.

"When we introduce the SUV, it will be a small car with some special design features but it will be instantly recognizable as a Smart and that is what we are working on right now."

This will include the Smart DNA: Two tone color, the combination of steel and plastic, interior textiles use and the unique shape and features of the instrument panels.

Wawra added: "We have to look at all the expectations consumers have for an SUV and apply them to our brand. At the moment people in the United States have no expectation of what Smart is."

In January this year Smart started production of its first four-seater, the forfour, in Born, the Netherlands, a plant shared with Mitsubishi.

Back in Smartville, things have moved on since the plant opened in 1998 producing just one model with 250 part numbers and a choice of four colors for the plastic body panels.

Now with the Smart fortwo and cabrio plus the Roadster and Coupe, there are 2,000 part numbers and much more complexity in the number of specifications.

"We have grown up very quickly," says Plant Manager Klaus Fischinger. "We have now gotten used to working with our supplier partners and have refined and optimized the manufacturing process."

It has not always been easy. The idea of sharing the assembly responsibility with supplier partners was revolutionary and has been ultimately successful, but Fischinger said there were doubts in the beginning.

"Each company has its own philosophy and each was worried as to how that would correspond. We meet every month to discuss how we have been doing and how we plan to work in the following month."

Smartville employs around 2,200 people. Hambach was chosen because DaimlerChrysler wanted the plant located in the middle of Western Europe. The plant is 6.2 mi. from the German border and it is an area that has changed nationalities several times through history. While 95 percent of the staff are French, most speak German.

Total investment in the plant stands at more than $650 million, including all systems suppliers. Wages in Smartville are the same whether you work for Smart or one of its partners, only the benefits may be different.

Body panels are produced by Dynamit Nobel where General Manager Hartmut Hensel boasts that there is virtually no waste. Plastic is recycled and used on black parts which are not seen on the car while even the paint changes are used to create some of the

Courtesy of Michael A. Messina

The Smart car, especially popular with European drivers, will debut in the United States as a four-seater in 2006.

weird and wonderful dual colours for some of Smart's unique body panels—this negates the need to completely clean out the paint tanks at the end of each color run.

Between 10 and 12 percent of all panels made are for the after-market or replacement—not necessarily because they are damaged, but so that people can change the color of their car. A complete set of panels costs around $600 and can be changed within 35 minutes—all you need is a screwdriver.

Another innovation is that nothing actually belongs to Smart until the car is signed off the line. It is when the bar code is scanned that suppliers are paid.

Theoretically the factory owns the car for just a few minutes before responsibility is handed to Mosolf the distribution logistics provider. In fact the plant usually hangs onto the vehicles for a day to give it a re-work buffer.

One part of Smartville's quirks will definitely not make it to the United States: There is no air conditioning at the plant because it's bad for the environment.

Although a special airflow system helps keep things bearable in mid-summer, last year's heatwave in France did mean the glass lifts which run up the outside of the building had to be sealed off.

If anyone had got stuck in one they would literally have become a French Fry.

Car Makers Zooming in on Youth

BY MATT NAUMAN
SAN JOSE MERCURY NEWS, JUNE 6, 2003

Outside of True, a hip-hop clothing store on once-hippie Haight Street in San Francisco, 18-year-old college student Thomas Estrada stepped forward to check out the new car designed for his generation.

Gen Y, meet Scion.

Scion, from Toyota, targets Generation Y—the emerging group of consumers now 9 to 23 years old. It's just one of a new breed designed for the younger crowd.

What makes a Gen Y car?

They're smaller, cheaper, faster and—with a lot of speakers—louder.

"I think it's cool, something different," said Estrada, who drives a 2001 Nissan Xterra sport-utility.

Scion, which goes on sale in California next week, tries hard to be trendy without seeming to try too hard. Other car makers are building heavily accessorized cars, like those featured in the *2 Fast 2 Furious* film sequel that opens today.

Both are aimed squarely at a generation—of 63 million—that buys only 5 percent of new cars now, but will buy 25 percent by 2010 and 40 percent by 2020.

"Boomers have long been the dominant generation that most marketers have targeted during the past 20 to 30 years," said Brian Bolain, Scion's sales promotions manager. "That's all about to change."

While Toyota's multimillion-dollar Scion experiment is the most radical move—it's a new franchise but the cars will be sold through existing Toyota dealerships—it's certainly not the only push toward hooking Gen Y buyers.

Other Efforts

Honda, already one of the most popular brands with young buyers due to its affordable, reliable and easily customized Civic, put the Element sport-utility on sale earlier this year. Billed as a dorm room on wheels, its ungainly profile allows maximum flexibility inside.

Dodge added horsepower to its Neon compact sedan, creating the SRT-4 that is sold as the quickest production car under $20,000.

Article by Matt Nauman from the *San Jose Mercury News* June 6, 2003. Copyright © *San Jose Mercury News*. All rights reserved. Reprinted with permission.

Mazda just released a 2003.5 version of its Mazda Speed Protege, a $20,000 small sedan that seems to have emerged from a tuner shop with its loud stereo, rear wing and fancy wheels.

Researchers identify several car brands—VW, Saturn, Hyundai, Jeep, Suzuki, Nissan, Mazda and Pontiac—as doing well with the youngest buyers, mainly because they offer affordable products with at least a bit of cool quotient.

Toyota, which sold more cars than anyone except Ford in 2002, is seen as moving in the wrong direction.

"Our cars tend to be more Mom and Dad cars," said Steve Cornelius, a San Jose Toyota dealer who started selling cars in 1976. "The big concern was we were turning into Oldsmobile."

So, next week, Cornelius will open Stevens Creek Scion in a separate facility from his Toyota store. It'll have the high-tech look and feel that will be Scion's signature, with computer kiosks to provide information and a 50-inch plasma TV to set the tone with music and images.

Researchers identify several car brands . . . as doing well with the youngest buyers, mainly because they offer affordable products with at least a bit of cool quotient.

Toyota has spent much time and money in researching Gen Y. It quickly found that they don't like to be marketed to, said Bolain. So, working with the San Francisco office of Attik, a British advertising agency, Toyota executives created a plan heavy on not being heavy-handed with a strong Internet component, plenty of so-called guerrilla marketing and lots of partnerships with trendy magazines.

"It's critical that Gen Y buyers be allowed to discover things, like new brands, at their own pace," Bolain said.

That's why nobody stepped in front of Estrada, the San Francisco State student, when he walked on Haight Street. He wandered over to see what was up with these cars he hadn't seen before.

The people doing the talking didn't look as if they worked for a big car company, like Toyota.

One had dreadlocks. All wore Adidas shirts, jackets, shoes and pants that look right in step on the street.

"It totally makes sense for them to come out with a car for their future generation of customers," said Barbara Coulon, vice president of trends at Youth Intelligence, a New York market-research firm focusing on the under-35-year-old market. "Mitsubishi and VW already have that hipper, younger feel."

Echoed Mike Bush, who edits the Youth Markets Alerts newsletter, "The less it feels like marketing, the better chance a company has with striking a chord with this group."

That's why a Scion was on display when music-magazine XLR8R (pronounced "accelerator") celebrated the holidays at a Colma bowling alley.

Toyota seems to understand that they need to make the Scion desirable, said Andrew Smith, XLR8R's publisher.

"Beyond Function"

"It's got to go beyond mere function if you're talking about reaching a hip, urban crowd," Smith said.

Something bigger is going on with the birth of Scion—the evolution of branding, said Chris Cedergren, analyst with Iceology, an automotive research firm in Thousand Oaks.

Two decades ago, it was thought that a strong brand would stay strong with each passing generation.

"That's no longer the case," he said. "Brands now have to continue to evolve their image not only to keep loyal buyers, but to attract new buyers."

B. J. Birtwell, Chrysler's youth marketing manager, applauds Toyota for trying Scion but says his company's Dodge SRT-4, a fast, affordable car is an equally valid approach. The success of *The Fast and the Furious* proves it. The mostly young owners of sport compact cars spent more than $2.3 billion on parts (not including wheels) in 2002, up 440 percent since 1998, and automakers want in on that action.

"The brands that are going to be on top will have a unique and complete understanding of this future consumer," Birtwell said. "As popular culture continues to embrace cars as part of who the youth is, I see this market continuing to grow. It used to be just about growing fast. Now it's going fast and looking good while you're doing it."

Lost? Let the Car Be Your Guide

T. EDWARD PHILLIPS
THE NEW YORK SUN, APRIL 8, 2004

The makers of Global Positioning Systems don't claim to save relationships. But that just might be a side benefit: Even when a driver decides to take an unplanned "shortcut," a navigation system in a GPS-equipped car will automatically reroute travel plans—thus eliminating debate over whether or not to stop at the gas station and ask for directions.

"It's kind of like having a passenger in the back seat who always knows where he is," said a spokesperson for the Consumer Electronics Association, Matt Swanston. New systems have full-color maps, they talk, and some have voice recognition software, he said. "The mega-trend is just the variety of choices you have now."

All major automakers now offer GPS navigation options for some or all of their new cars, and it is fast becoming a standard feature for luxury models. But getting a system for an older car is a snap. Aftermarket systems—products or services added after the sale of the car—come as either portable models that plug into the cigarette lighter or as permanent systems installed in the car stereo slot. A driver's ideal system depends on a his or her budget and preferences.

A friend and I tried out a portable Magellan system on a trip from Cobble Hill, Brooklyn, to the East Village. Like nearly all GPS systems, it displayed a map of the city that moved in real time as the car progressed on its journey. Programming the route was easy. After it located a (much needed) gas station along the way, it identified the destination, Tompkins Square Park, and plotted a route. When my friend decided to take the Brooklyn Bridge instead of the Manhattan Bridge, the system devised a new route after about a minute.

GPS has become so prevalent that it's easy to forget that this technology was originally developed for the military. The current system, consisting of 24 satellites that emit radio signals as they orbit the earth, was completed in 1994. A GPS receiver calculates its location by triangulating its distance between two satellites whose exact position is known, thanks to ground stations that track them.

Global Positioning System software then translates that data into information we can use. Nearly all the GPS systems available in this country use Navteq data. This Chicago based company has

Article by T. Edward Phillips from *The New York Sun* April 8, 2004. Reprinted by permission of *The New York Sun* © 2004.

mapped 40 countries so far; maps are updated as new roads and ramps are built. If you've ever looked up an address online using-Mapquest.com, you've used Navteq data.

One useful feature that all of the systems share is something called "points of interest." This allows the driver to locate the nearest gas stations, pharmacies, restaurants, parks, and hospitals, among other sites. Another common feature are voice prompts that warn the driver of upcoming turns.

> *Some versions of the navigation systems are car manufacturers' aftermarket add-ons.*

The easiest and least expensive option for your car is a portable unit like those offered by Magellan and Garmin International. They are cheaper than most of the versions that require installation, and can be moved from car to car—a boon to a family with several cars. The systems plug into a car's cigarette lighter.

The Magellan Roadmate 700 sells for $1,299 and is small enough to fit into a large coat pocket. Its touch-screen menus are intuitive, and after about five minutes of tinkering, a beginner should be able to program in a destination.

Like the Roadmate, Garmin's StreetPilot 2620 has maps of the entire U.S. on its hard drive. It was released in March for $1,516 and includes a few extra features, like a way to specify areas to avoid in case of road construction or bad traffic, as well as a remote control for the passenger. The StreetPilot stores 5 million points of interest compared to the Magellan's 2 million.

If those features aren't enough, more powerful systems that run off DVDs can be professionally installed. These systems contain more than 10 million points of interest. Some of these systems include voice-recognition technology, though it hasn't yet reached the point where you can simply tell the car where you want to go. Instead, the driver must use a limited number of verbal commands.

The Pioneer AVIC-N1 begins shipping this month for $2,000 and combines an audio-visual system with navigation. The user keys in the location on a touch screen. The system is an all-in-one that plays audio CDs, picks up satellite radio, and can play DVDs for the kids in the back seat. Since the mapping DVD has to be removed while other CDs or DVDs are played, it stores the route in its memory. Kenwood and Alpine also make popular versions of the aftermarket navigation systems.

Options from car manufacturers add between $1,000 to $2,000 to a vehicle's price. Some versions of the navigation systems are car manufacturers' aftermarket add-ons, but as GPS becomes more standard, the systems are more and more fully integrated into the car.

The latest models from BMW and Mercedes, for example, feature control buttons on the steering wheel. Directions are provided under the speedometer instead of off to the side, so the driver doesn't need to turn his head. These systems also have voice recognition. The new BMW 545 even includes an option for a headsup display that projects information right onto the windshield.

"It's reaching the point in the auto industry that cars without navigation systems will be an oddity," said a salesman at BMW of Manhattan, Richard Pettinella. Like so many revolutionary technologies that came before, GPS is on track to become fully integrated in our lives; our children will find it hard to believe there was a time when we actually got lost on the road.

III. Traffic and Safety

Editors' Introduction

T he statistics are not cheerful. Today, a motor vehicle accident occurs every second, killing between 800,000 and one million people per year worldwide. Traffic-related injuries may be as high as 50 million yearly. In the United States alone, traffic accidents are the leading cause of death for individuals 35 and younger. The car has led to an estimated 18 million deaths since its creation. As a result, safety has become one of the highest priorities for motorists when choosing their vehicles. Drivers want front and side air bags, four-wheel drive, anti-lock brakes . . . the complete litany of safety features offered in the advertisements.

In his article "Safety First," Daniel A. Thomas addresses some of these very issues, proposing that more thorough training for drivers would help decrease accidents, but he acknowledges the difficulty of making human beings modify their habits. If people cannot correct their behavior as drivers, at least automakers can install better, more useful technology in their cars. He anticipates additions such as night vision systems that will allow drivers to see more in the dark, radar technology to detect vehicles in blind spots, and automatic braking and steering systems that could kick into action upon determining that a collision is imminent. Even something as basic as traffic signs could be improved, Thomas suggests.

Other safety features that are becoming quite popular are communication and tracking systems that utilize GPS (global positioning system) to identify cars and their locations at all times. Often, these systems are exceptionally useful, allowing drivers to get help with directions or find a stolen car (or even a misplaced vehicle in a vast parking lot). Diane Katz examines both the pros and cons of such tracking devices in "As Technology Advances, So Do Privacy Concerns." Some drivers, such as James Turner, who sued Acme Rent-a-Car for tracking him without his knowledge and fining him for speeding, see it as an invasion of privacy, an Orwellian Big Brother on the go. Meanwhile, in Diane Cadrain's article "States Cracking Down on Driving and Phoning," and Jeff Bennett's "In-car Electronics Can Distract, Imperil," the writers worry about the presence of other electronic and digital devices in vehicles. With an ever-expanding list of distractions, such as mobile phones, CD players, and navigation systems, drivers find their attention being divided, with potentially dangerous results. Cadrain notes that a variety of states are following the lead set by New York, New Jersey, and Washington, D.C., in passing legislation to ban the use of cell phones while driving, while Bennett reports on concerns by automakers such as GM and Ford about the liabilities that phones and other electronic devices can pose for drivers of their cars.

Ann Job, however, suggests that another piece of equipment is necessary in vehicles: a rearview camera or sensor. In "Blind Spots, Backover Dangers Gain Attention" Job writes of the growing threat of injuries or even fatalities due to drivers backing up their vehicles without being able to see objects or people in their blind spots. Approximately 2,767 people were taken to emergency rooms due to backover incidents between July 2000 and June 2001 and, with the increased popularity of larger vehicles like SUVs, the size of the blind spot grows with the car.

Children, due to their short stature, are often the victims of backup accidents but are not out of danger even if they safely make it into the car. In her article entitled "A Parent's Lapse Can Be Fatal in the Summer Heat," Jeanne Wright warns against leaving children in closed vehicles during the summer months, when temperatures inside cars quickly skyrocket. She reports that, during the summer of 2003, a record 42 children died nationwide after being left in locked cars. Even normally attentive parents may occasionally forget their children, especially if the kids are seated in the back seat of a large auto or SUV, but the results can be fatal. Wright quotes meteorologist and professor Jan Null with the warning, "Parents and caregivers need to get the word that a car is not a babysitter . . . but it can easily become an oven." Yet another danger to children comes from air bags, as presented in the sidebar entitled "Children and Air Bags."

Incidents such as these and many others are not the fault of the vehicle, as Richard Rubin explains in his article, "SUV Capable, But What About Driver?" It seems that drivers are often overconfident in their SUVs; putting their faith in four-wheel drive and sheer bulk, SUV owners sometimes drive recklessly and cause accidents. Why might drivers be reckless in the first place? One reason is discussed in a report by the National Highway Traffic Safety Administration (NHTSA) entitled "National Survey of Drinking and Driving Attitudes and Behaviors, 2001." According to the NHTSA, the long-standing problem of drunk driving has not gone away.

In an attempt to discourage reckless driving, accident-provoking anger, and general vehicular stress, Jessie Milligan offers tips on how to become "the Zen commuter," a relaxed, calm, and competent individual who can handle the anxiety of driving. Milligan and experts on driving psychology urge drivers to breathe deeply, think positively, and accept unavoidable situations gracefully. And it couldn't hurt to toss in some aromatherapy or massage cushions, either.

Safety First

By Daniel A. Thomas
PLANNING, MAY 2004

Automobiles allow people greater choice in housing location and ability to travel or commute easily. However, this freedom comes with a significant risk of accidents and the trauma and loss of productivity they cause.

The National Highway Traffic Safety Administration estimates that in 2002 highway crashes accounted for $230.6 billion ($820 per person) in costs associated with medical treatment, rehabilitation, police and legal services, property damage, insurance, disability and workers compensation, lost productivity, and social services for those who cannot return to work.

In 2002, a traffic accident occurred nearly every three seconds and fatalities increased to 42,815, the highest level since 1990. A December 2003 NHTSA study revealed that motor vehicle accidents were the leading cause of deaths for people between the ages of four and 33 and the eighth most frequent cause of death for all age ranges. If traffic fatalities were viewed as a social illness, people would be calling it an epidemic.

The good news is that the 2002 fatality rate was the lowest since records were first established in 1975. And although there were 2.92 million crash-related injuries—one for every resident of the city of Chicago—this was also a historic low level. NHTSA attributes the decrease to improved vehicle design, vehicle safety features, and more stringent federal safety standards.

These figures are of particular interest to planners. The spread of urbanization, continued dependence on the automobile, and changing U.S. demographics mean that these trends are not likely to be reversed in the near future. Road safety will continue to be an issue.

What's the Answer?

One way to reduce accidents is to design our environment so that people will drive less. Transit-oriented development, neo-traditional neighborhoods, providing access to transit, and constructing infrastructure for nonmotorized transportation are all ways to accomplish that. However, they are not likely to have significant effect.

Article by Daniel A. Thomas from *Planning* May 2004. Copyright © *Planning*. Reprinted with permission.

Better Signs

While roads have been engineered to improve user safety, there have also been recent improvements that make signs more understandable and thus make roads safer. To be effective, signs must be easily seen, information must be clearly and directly presented, and the driver must understand the message. When any of these elements are compromised, the result can be delayed decisions, potentially erratic driving maneuvers, and possible errors.

To avoid such problems:

- Make sure symbols are understandable, especially for older drivers. Many symbols are standard in the Manual on Uniform Traffic Control Devices (MUTCD), but a slight redesign may make the message easier to understand.

- Design signs so there is significant contrast between the symbol and the background and symbols are not crowded.

- Use a larger text font so messages can be recognized earlier.

- Hang illuminated street signs from overhead mast arms. Such signs, widely used in Florida, are easier to read from a distance and at night than typical street signs. They help motorists to determine their location as they enter an intersection.

- Post street signs in advance of intersections to give drivers a chance to make careful turning decisions and to make the lane selection safely in advance of an intersection.

- Use Clearview font to make the text more legible. The current standard highway font recommended by MUTCD is Highway Gothic. But Clearview maximizes the space between letters, thus reducing the "irradiation" or "halation" phenomenon (the bleeding of letters under illumination at night).

- Do not present too much information on a sign. At high speeds, drivers cannot easily process too much information, especially if they are unfamiliar with an area.

- Be clear. Do not leave the driver uncertain about the intent of a message on a sign.

Another answer is to encourage better drivers. Ninety percent of accidents are attributable to human error, according to Drive for Life, a coalition of highway safety experts and advocates. The five most common driving mistakes are: failing to pay attention, driving while drowsy, driver distraction, failing to adjust to adverse weather conditions, and driving aggressively.

Changing human behavior is not easy, however. That leaves the third solution: Making automobiles safer, something engineers have been working on since the invention of the automobile. To date most of their efforts have been focused on passive safety technology—seatbelts, for instance, and automobiles that absorb impacts to protect occupants.

The next generation of safety technology focuses on active technology that will help other motorists to control their cars, react faster to other drivers, and boost concentration. These are some of the safety features that are already in showrooms or anticipated soon.

- Radar technology to detect vehicles in blind spots during a lane change. Blind spots are a particular problem in SUVs and minivans. With radar technology, borrowed from military applications, an audio signal or a light will alert the driver to traffic approaching from the rear.

- Crash warning systems. Another kind of radar technology allows the vehicle to "see" and to estimate the likelihood of potential traffic threats. A warning signal will give the driver time to maneuver in order to avoid a collision. These systems may be coupled with active braking systems.

- Adaptive cruise control. ACC is similar to conventional cruise control, but is uses radar to monitor the headway interval and maintain a safe distance from the car ahead. When the gap narrows, the system emits an audible warning or initiates a braking maneuver.

- Active braking systems. Brakes are automatically applied when radar determines that a collision is imminent—for example, if a car is approaching at a high rate of speed. In the future, the system might include an active steering system that would automatically begin an evasive action.

- Lane departure warning. LDW systems are a way to combat sleepy or inattentive drivers. The system uses tiny cameras or other monitors to scan lane markers, guardrails, and other roadside barriers. It identifies a vehicle's position in relation to lane markings and sounds a warning when a vehicle begins to veer off the road. Already included in some commercial trucks, it is anticipated to be installed in cars within the next couple of years.

- Attention control. The attention control system uses a camera to monitor the frequency and duration of eyelid movement. If it detects signs of sleepiness, the system will warn the driver ahead of time to take a break until fully attentive.

- Adaptive forward lighting. The new lighting system can vary the length, width, and direction of headlight beams. The headlights swivel to either side to light up intersections and tight corners. When the low beam is on, the system directs the light to the direction in which the vehicle is moving.

- Sign recognition. The traffic sign recognition system uses a digital display to alert drivers to applicable road signs.

- Night vision. Under development in different forms by various automobile manufacturers, night vision will improve a driver's ability to see and judge potential roadway hazards. Ford's Night-Eye vision system uses a low-light camera to warn the driver of threats that cannot be seen with the naked eye. A system developed by Mercedes Benz projects images onto a right-hand display. Infrared laser headlights illuminate drivers to spot hazards much earlier.

Volkswagon places sensors in the front of the car to detect heat generated from objects ahead or to the side, including trees, parked cars, and animals. Thermal energy images are converted into digital signals and projected on the windshield.

Older Drivers

As the American population ages, planners are focusing more attention on the special needs of the elderly. According to Census Bureau population projections, by 2030 one in every five Americans (70.2 million people) will be 65 or older. That figure is sure to have an impact on all aspects of roadway safety.

Getting more older drivers to understand their changing abilities may be the first step in improving their safety.

Age takes a toll on vision, hearing, physical strength, and cognitive skills. Driving suffers as a result, with decreased reaction time and range of motion, and a decline in peripheral vision. Difficulties are exacerbated when older drivers must function in stressful situations or under the effect of medication.

Older drivers are thus more likely than younger ones to misjudge oncoming traffic speeds and distances or to fail to see other drivers in their vicinity. They are more likely to be involved in multi-vehicle crashes, and to have difficulty merging with high-speed traffic and changing lanes on congested streets.

Statistics show that drivers age 65 and older are relatively safe motorists, with fewer accidents per 1,000 licensed drivers than most other age groups. But starting at age 70, the risk increases, and it goes way up at 80, with fatalities far more frequent.

Many older drivers recognize their diminishing driving skills. They limit their time on the road and drive when they feel the safest—avoiding rush hours, driving shorter distances, refraining from driving in poor weather or at night. They drive fewer miles on average than any other age group.

Getting more older drivers to understand their changing abilities may be the first step in improving their safety. Some states are requiring older drivers to take driving tests more often to determine if they still possess the physical and cognitive skills needed to be safe drivers.

The high-tech safety devices described above may help to prevent some accidents involving older drivers. But low-tech solutions can also contribute to safety. These include: having good acceleration to merge into traffic, getting anti-lock brakes to improve stopping

What's Available Now

Dealers are already marketing devices, including backup cameras, to solve the problem of blind spots in minivans and SUVs with poor rear-end visibility. Side-mounted traffic-view cameras are also available for the passenger side to help alert the driver to pedestrians, bicycles, and merging vehicles. Most of these devices are available only in high-end cars, however, and are not standard equipment.

Radar systems are currently used to detect objects in front of or behind vehicles and to assist in gauging distance during parking maneuvers. Coming soon is a next-generation backup camera that will enhance visibility under varying lighting conditions.

More for SUVs: Rollovers have been a serious safety concern. New electronic stability control (ESC) systems monitor steering wheel position, tire speed, centrifugal forces, and other driving conditions. If the system reveals that the driver is about to lose control, microprocessors automatically apply individual brakes or reduce engine power to reduce the chance of skids, spin-outs, and rollovers. Toyota reports that ESC reduced single-vehicle crashes in Japan by 35 percent and head-on crashes by 30 percent.

To combat driver distraction, automobile manufacturers have developed, hands-free voice systems to control heating and cooling, and entertainment systems as well as cellular phones. An advanced-design, voice-operated control system and an ultrasound-based driver-information system target the sound—traffic news and so on—without disturbing passengers.

Also aimed at driver concentration: Telematics systems that combine vehicle control and monitoring capabilities with location tracking, and wireless telecommunications. GM's OnStar system, a subscription-based service, and other telematic services provide emergency assistance (e.g., remote diagnostics that monitor critical components in the vehicle), remote door unlocking, air bag deployment notification, and tracking of stolen vehicles. Drivers can add such convenience features as Internet access and cellular telephone service, and they can obtain information about routes, parking, and hotels.

By 2006, nearly all vehicles will have advanced air bags that deploy with different levels of force depending on how hard you crash and whether occupants are buckled up. Sensors will prevent passenger air bags from deploying if a small child is in a seat. Many 2004 models already have this feature.

Ignition interlocks are aimed at reducing the incidence of drunk driving. Some states already require ignition interlocks on automobiles of repeat DUI offenders. To start the vehicle, drivers must breathe into a tube to measure their blood-alcohol content.

To improve pedestrian safety, some automobiles are being provided with an energy impact absorption system designed to reduce the impact on the walker in the event of a crash. The secret is to increase the space between the engine and car hood so that in the event of a collision, the hood absorbs the impact. These systems are already fairly common in Europe.

time, having a car that is a bright color or has daytime running lights so it is more easily seen by other drivers, and having adjustable seats that make it easier to see obstacles ahead and to maintain a safe distance from deploying airbags.

Transportation planners can play an important role in designing roads that consider the increasing number of older drivers and their safety. The lettering, color, size, and location of traffic signs can be changed to significantly improve visibility and communication with the driver. Illuminated overhead street signs, wider driving lanes, and improved lighting will also improve the driving environment. Rumble strips to avoid lane drift may be recommended in certain areas, but they can be a deterrent to on-street bicycling and therefore create other safety issues.

Too Technology-Dependent?

Engineers and automobile manufacturers continue to make our driving environment safer. There is a concern, however, that new technologies will lull drivers into a false sense of security, and the human factor will overcome these advancements.

> *There is a concern ... that new technologies will lull drivers into a false sense of security.*

For example, a common misconception among SUV owners is that four-wheel drive covers all the safety bases in foul weather. Some SUV owners may drive more aggressively as a result, depending on the traction of their vehicle to set them straight on icy roads and size to protect them in collisions.

But four-wheel drive boosts traction only during a straight-line acceleration. When turning or stopping, it does almost nothing to improve stability or safety. In addition, there are many anecdotes about drivers depending on the ability of anti-lock brakes to stop their vehicles to avoid a crash. It may not work.

No computer-based safety technology is fail-safe. It is nearly impossible for a computer to predict human behavior in every instance and to take the correct evasive action. There are also human components of safe driving that are out of reach of computer intelligence.

For example, a human driver is likely to recognize that the figure at the side of the road is a child, who might dart into the street at any moment. To a computer, the child is identical to a short adult. Similarly, it's the driver not the computer who realizes that the cyclist who has not yet started to decelerate has seen you, is intending to stop, and will not plow into the intersection. In addition, some road hazards, such as black ice, cannot yet be sensed by computers.

Bottom Line

No matter how safe the vehicle is, the way it's driven will determine the extent of an injury. Drivers need to pay attention to the road, select cars that maximize their ability to see and understand roadway conditions, and use but not depend on technological advancements to prevent accidents and injuries.

As Technology Advances, So Do Privacy Concerns

By Diane Katz
The Detroit News, December 2, 2001

James Turner was 300 miles from home and low on gas when his debit card was rejected at a self-serve pump. "What is going on?" he wondered. There should have been a few hundred bucks in his account.

A telephone call to the bank both clarified matters and left Turner cold. His account, the teller informed him, had been electronically emptied by the Connecticut rental car company he regularly patronized.

Turner's saga subsequently captured national headlines and earned the New Haven theater manager the sympathy of those who likewise feel preyed upon by untamed technology. Nestled beneath the hood of Turner's rented minivan was an unseen black box that monitored his every press of the pedal and turn of the wheel as he traveled to and from Norfolk, Va., for a gospel performance of *Can a Woman Make a Man Lose His Mind?*

All the data on his comings and goings were relayed via satellite to a computer at Acme Rent-a-Car. And after Turner was twice clocked driving 78 mph and once at 83 mph while traversing three states, the company levied $450 in speeding fines—promptly charged to his debit card.

"I was angry, shocked, in disbelief," says Turner, who insists that he didn't fully comprehend the contract fine print advising customers that Acme cars are "GPS equipped" and that "Vehicles driven in excess of posted speed limits will be charged $150 per occurrence."

The dizzying array of electronic devices capable of monitoring people's every move has many Americans plenty edgy about a loss of privacy. The concern has been magnified in the aftermath of the September 11 terrorist attacks, as Congress has vastly expanded the government's surveillance powers.

Whether Americans condemn or celebrate the new technologies seems to depend largely on the degree of control at their disposal. But there's no agreement among policymakers or the public about how best to maximize that power. Or what may become of society if they don't.

Reprinted with permission from *The Detroit News*.

"I thought a GPS system was a screen in a car that you can program a destination and it will tell you how to get there," Turner says.

That it is. But it's also much more. "GPS" is shorthand for global positioning system, which uses radio waves to exchange location information with a spray of 24 satellites rotating the Earth. Developed for military use in the 1980s, the technology was released for commercial use in 1995 and has since been adapted to a variety of navigational applications, principally in motor vehicles.

> *"This is a gross misuse of technology."*—**James Turner**

Such human tracking makes the electronic droppings of people's every mouse click the least of America's privacy worries, watchdogs warn. Technology has advanced to the point that the Digital Angel "biosensor," a watch-like wrist device, can monitor key body functions such as pulse, temperature and blood oxygen levels and download our inner workings to most any desk-top computer. The next generation of Angels will track glucose and blood pressure, too, and the company has secured a patent for implantable sensors.

Chicago attorney Daniel R. Sovocool, who specializes in privacy law, likens such real-time tracking to "'cookies' on sterioids."

"It's a scary feeling to know that someone knows where you are at any given moment," Turner says. "This is a gross misuse of technology."

But is it? GPS and other so-called telematics tools also can yield enormous economic and public safety benefits. By keeping closer tabs on rental vehicles, for example, fewer cars are stolen or crashed. That in turn lowers insurance premiums for companies like Acme—which then can discount rental rates.

"Most people think it's great because we specialize in low rates," says Acme attorney Max Brunswick. "And people know if we rent to speeders, good drivers are going to be subsidizing bad drivers."

Robert Lautenback was similarly motivated to invest in telematics for his Thrifty Car franchise in Grand Rapids. His online testimonial endorsing the tracking products of Ontario-based AirIQ Inc. states: "(It) has empowered me to know exactly where my vehicle has been, at what time, and at what speed it was traveling. Now that's powerful."

Consumers need not understand every engineering nuance of the technology to know it will cost them to speed. Those who prefer higher rates to prying eyes can simply take their business elsewhere, telematics enthusiasts advise.

Sales of GPS devices for passenger cars totaled nearly $1 billion last year and are projected to exceed $10 billion by 2004, when an estimated 90 percent of new vehicles will be so equipped.

Pros and Cons of Electronic Tracking

Benefits
- Influences people to behave appropriately, resulting in lower costs for companies and lower prices for consumers.
- Allows the compilation of personal information, such as health conditions, which could help in emergencies.
- Gives your whereabouts to family.

Disadvantages
- Allows outsiders to track your every movement, which could result in unauthorized exploitation.
- May not result in positive change of behavior.
- In the hands of government or private firms, could violate privacy concerns and constitutional liberties.

The technology already is widely used by trucking firms to monitor freight movements. Insurers, meanwhile, are experimenting with telematics to adjust rates by the minute. Ohio-based Progressive Casualty Insurance Group, for example, is tracking the driving habits of consenting clients and adjusting premiums accordingly—netting drivers savings ranging from 5 to 30 percent.

"Black box" data also is proving useful as legal evidence. Mary Louise Middleton, 77, claimed sudden acceleration sent her car plowing through the plate-glass window of the Waxahachie, Texas, post office, fatally pinning Mildred Menges, 71, to a wall. Data retrieved from the engine sensors in Middleton's Cadillac ultimately discounted that claim and helped the victim's daughters to prevail in the wrongful death suit they filed.

Since 1994, General Motors Corp. vehicles have been wired to collect data on deceleration, airbags, and nine other systems. As of 1999, the black boxes also began recording brake and throttle status as well as velocity, and additional measurements are likely to follow. Other automakers have installed similar but more limited surveillance technology.

Turner is suing Acme for invasion of privacy, while Connecticut's Consumer Protection Division has filed an unfair trade practice complaint.

"What we're really hoping for is full disclosure," says Bernadette Keyes, Turner's attorney. "In order for the contract to be valid, there must have been a 'meeting of the minds.'"

Whether the language in Acme's rental agreement was sufficient for Turner to make an informed decision is strictly a matter of contract law. More broadly, privacy advocates are lobbying aggressively for new government controls on the commercial collection and exchange of electronic data. But whether stricter regulation would enhance or diminish individuals' control of personal data is hotly contested.

The Center for Democracy and Technology, for example, favors federal legislation to codify privacy standards and provide remedies against "bad actors."

"In particular," says Jerry Berman, the center's executive director, "baseline legislation . . . would assure individuals consistent application of principles of fair information practices and an effective redress mechanism."

Hundreds of privacy measures are pending in state legislatures as well. But to the extent regulation centralizes control over the flow of information, individuals would exercise less direct authority over personal data and, say its opponents, become vulnerable to a false sense of security.

Jim Harper, editor of Privacilla.org, an online privacy think tank, instead advocates more personalized remedies. A scarcity of privacy, he argues, will make protection technologies more marketable. For

---

"All privacy laws will accomplish is to provide common folk with a warm, fuzzy mirage of seclusion."—David Brin, futurist

---

$60 a year, web users can now purchase "anonymizing" services from companies such as Zero-Knowledge, which will encrypt communications, block unsolicited mail and shield one's surfing habits from surveillance.

"In a country like ours, where hundreds of millions of people are making billions of decisions every day that affect what happens with their personal information, the guesses of politicians and bureaucrats cannot possibly accommodate the actual privacy preferences of consumers," Harper says.

"The way to protect privacy," he adds, "is to distribute those decisions to the people who are affected by them the most."

Besides, argues futurist David Brin, privacy is impossible to maintain in an open society.

"All privacy laws will accomplish is to provide common folk with a warm, fuzzy mirage of seclusion, while having the major effect of preventing you from finding out anything at all about the rich and powerful," says Brin.

"Perhaps, after all is said and done," he adds, "most of us will even decide that it's better to know our neighbors (in their multitudes) than to live a fiction, a lie, of splendid, lonely isolation."

The debate has largely focused on private-sector data collection. The number of employers monitoring e-mail or videotaping employees has doubled in the past four years, according to a survey by the

American Management Association. But most are more worried about protecting trade secrets and limiting liability than whether workers are surfing online sex sites.

But it is government that actually delves deepest into the personal lives of Americans, be it the Internal Revenue Service or law enforcement agencies.

The Privacy Foundation, for example, awarded its 2001 Big Brother award to the Federal Bureau of Investigation for its online snooping Carnivore program, while the U.S. Department of Health and Human Services ranked as runner-up for its sloppy handling of medical records.

Officials in Tampa, Fla., warranted special mention for their use of secret surveillance cameras equipped with face-recognition software to scan for felons and missing persons among an unsuspecting Super Bowl crowd. Similar screening technology is being installed in several major airports, including Boston, Oakland, Calif., and Providence, R.I. Sales of biometric software, in fact, are projected to surge from $165 million in 2000 to $2.5 billion by decade's end.

Local officials around the country also are mounting electronic eyes over roadways and intersections to nab scofflaws in the act— which helps increase municipal revenues.

But Americans may not necessarily be so easily subdued. "It will change behavior, but not necessarily in ways we can anticipate," says author Virginia Postrel. "It is not as simple as being watched and being good."

Editors' note: In February 2002 a hearing officer in the state of Connecticut recommended that Acme Rent-a-Car be barred from using GPS technology for tracking and penalizing speeding customers. The decision was upheld by Connecticut's commissioner of the Department of Consumer Protection, James Fleming.

States Cracking Down on Driving and Phoning

By Diane Cadrain
HR Magazine, April 2004

State legislatures are putting the brakes on people who use cell phones while driving. New Jersey is the third major jurisdiction in the nation, after New York and the District of Columbia, to pass a law barring the driver of a moving vehicle from talking on a handheld cell phone.

The dangers of workers becoming distracted by conversations are especially disturbing for employers because companies that issue cell phones to their employees risk liability for injuries caused by those who drive while doing business.

Here's a look at the laws on the books and proposed, the potential for personal injury liability, and the implications for company policies on cell phone use.

- The New Jersey law, which will take effect in July, bars the use of handheld phones by drivers of moving vehicles except in emergencies. It's punishable by fines ranging from $100 to $250. Lawmakers made it a secondary action, though: Police may ticket for cell phone use only in conjunction with stopping a driver for another offense. The law pre-empts several local ordinances.

- The D.C. City Council this year barred the use of handheld electronic devices while operating a motor vehicle. If signed by Mayor Anthony Williams and approved by Congress, the bill takes effect in July.

- New York state enacted the nation's first statewide ban on driving while talking on a handheld cell phone, effective Dec. 1, 2001. The law is punishable by a $100 fine, and, like the New Jersey law, it preempts local laws and allows the use of hands-free devices.

More than two dozen localities in Florida, Massachusetts, New Jersey, New Mexico, New York, Ohio, Pennsylvania and Utah have enacted their own ordinances.

Reprinted with permission of *HR Magazine* published by the Society for Human Resources Management, Alexandria, VA.

Legislative Explosion

Since 1999, said Matt Sundeen, who monitors transportation issues for the Denver-based National Conference of State Legislatures, legislation on the issue has been introduced in every state. Last year alone, 42 states considered bills, and this year proposals are already on the table in at least 10 states.

But the fines under state and local laws are minor compared to the potential liability of hitting someone while talking on a company cell phone.

In Virginia, for example, law firm Cooley Godward is fighting a multimillion-dollar lawsuit brought by the family of a 15-year-old gift who was struck and killed by one of the firm's lawyers who, allegedly, was making business calls at the time.

Sundeen pointed out several other examples:

- **Arkansas.** Dykes Industries paid a $16.2 million settlement after a 78-year-old woman was struck and disabled by a Dykes salesman who was making a sales call.

- **Hawaii.** The state paid $1.5 million to a man who was hit by a state-employed teacher who had just finished using her cell phone on the way to work.

- **Pennsylvania.** Investment firm Smith Barney paid a $500,000 settlement to the family of a motorcyclist who was hit by a broker on a sales call.

Employers are generally liable for the negligence of employees who are traveling for work, attorneys say. If a cell phone was involved, the employer could try to show that use of the phone didn't cause the accident or that the employee was deviating from the job—for example, by making a purely personal call.

According to Sundeen, police have issued over 140,000 tickets under the New York law.

In New Jersey, the telecommunications industry is fairly positive about the new law. "We'd rather see no legislation at all," said Diane Rainey, public affairs manager for Nextel. "This law unfairly singles out cell phone use despite the existence of plenty of other distractions. But since it's now a law, we're encouraging our customers and employees to abide by it and buy hands-free equipment."

In-Car Electronics
Can Distract, Imperil

By Jeff Bennett
Detroit Free Press, October 26, 2000

The number of driving distractions in vehicles is steadily increasing.

There are six-disc CD players, cell phones and screens that allow drivers to get directions with the push of a button. These are conveniences that consumers have clamored for, but there's a growing debate over their safety.

"There is great excitement about the possibility of how these systems might enhance the driving experience," says a report released last week by Paul Green, a senior research scientist at the University of Michigan Transportation Research Institute.

"However, relatively little emphasis has been given to the potential risks associated with overload these systems might pose to drivers. If action is not taken a significant number of information system-related deaths and injuries will result," Green wrote.

Such injuries could cause a consumer backlash or prompt the federal government to step in and ban the use of many products in moving vehicles, he wrote. Some industry experts say automakers or the government must establish guidelines for types of devices added to vehicles.

Last week, leaders of General Motors Corp. and Ford Motor Co. called for new steps to stem driving distractions.

GM plans to launch a $10-million "SenseAble Driving" campaign to teach current and future motorists how to avoid being distracted at the wheel.

While motorists might think they spend a few seconds glancing at map screens in the dashboard, researchers and experts warn that more has to be done to keep drivers' eyes on the road.

In a recent test, the time to select a point of interest on a telematics display was more than a minute. That's three times longer than dialing a cell phone number, Green says.

Japan is one of few countries to conduct extensive research on driver distraction. In 1997 there were 2,095 injuries and 20 deaths caused by cell phones. Navigation-system distraction accounted for 117 injuries and one death.

In 1999, cell phone injuries jumped to 2,418 and 24 deaths while navigation injuries jumped to 205 and two deaths.

Article by Jeff Bennett, from the *Detroit Free Press* October 26, 2000. Copyright © *Detroit Free Press*. Reprinted with permission.

In America, a National Highway Transportation Safety Administration survey found 44 percent of drivers carry cell phones in vehicles. Of those, 7 percent have access to e-mail, and 3 percent can receive faxes.

NHTSA is doing research into the effects of voice-controlled systems and driver distractions in general. It has concluded that cell phone use increases the risk of an accident.

There are no industry guidelines or government regulations governing in-car computers, and the industry would prefer that regulators stay on the sidelines for now. Automakers said they want to put more emphasis on voice-activated devices so drivers won't get distracted looking at the dashboard.

But three research papers presented at Convergence 2000 electronics conference last week in Detroit suggest that voice-controlled systems pose serious safety concerns. In addition to Green's paper, there was one by Barry H. Kantowitz, another University of Michigan scientist, and a paper by four researchers from the University of Iowa.

An experiment conducted by the Iowa scientists showed that when e-mail was read to drivers, their response time to brake lights from a vehicle in front of them increased 30 percent.

Researchers don't want to ban electronic devices. They say navigation systems allow drivers to travel to unknown destinations in safety, avoiding the need to refer to paper maps. Mobile phones provide rapid access to emergency services.

Blind Spots, Backover
Dangers Gain Attention

By Ann Job
MSN Autos, June 23, 2003

Are you extra aware and alert when you're in the vicinity of a sport-utility vehicle, van or a pickup truck that's backing up?

Are you especially watchful for children when you're behind the wheel of a tall-riding vehicle—be it a van, truck or SUV—and you're backing it up?

You should be. According to *Consumer Reports*, the blind spot behind a tall vehicle such as a Chevrolet Avalanche truck can extend as much as 51 feet in the case of a small-stature driver about 5 feet 1 inches tall. Even for an average-sized driver, 5 feet 8 inches tall, the blind spot can extend nearly 30 feet behind the Avalanche, according to the consumer advice publication.

"No one is telling people there's a bigger blind spot in these vehicles," said Janette Fennell, founder and president of the child safety advocacy group Kids and Cars.

Pointing out her statistics showing at least one child a week in the United States is killed in a "backover" incident, Fennell urges that some kind of "backover warning and prevention device" be made mandatory on all vehicles.

Adults Can Be Hit, Too

Fennell's group only collects data on children, but she acknowledges adults also can be and are killed and injured in backovers.

In fact, the Centers for Disease Control and Prevention estimated 2,767 people were treated in emergency rooms from July 2000 through June 2001 because of backovers. "This is a huge problem," Fennell said. "A lot of [the problem] is due to the change in our vehicle mix" that has more people driving tall-profile vehicles, she said.

Indeed, Fennell's research indicates that "in 60 percent of the [backover] cases, it's a truck, van or SUV that's involved," Fennell said. The reduced rearward visibility is caused by the design and tall profile of SUVs, pickup trucks and even vans.

The top edge of the tailgates and liftgates in these vehicles typically sits high and so do the vehicles themselves. This means that unaware children and small-stature adults and anything not tall enough to be visible in the rear window glass might be run over as the vehicle is backing up.

Article by Ann Job from *MSN Autos* June 23, 2003. Copyright © *MSN Autos*. Reprinted with permission.

Blind Spots Not New

It's important to point out that even cars have blind spots—areas right at the back of a vehicle where a driver, even making good use of the rearview mirror and side mirrors, doesn't quite get full visibility.

"There's an area under the rear bumper where we just can't see that area," said Pamela LaBuhn, product engineer at General Motors Corp.

> *It's important to point out that even cars have blind spots.*

Many consumers would likely be surprised at just how large this area is, even in a car.

According to Consumers Union, a 5-foot-1 driver of a Honda Accord can experience a blind spot that extends 17 feet behind the car. For an average-sized driver of an Accord, the blind spot is approximately 13 feet long.

This is plenty of space to obscure objects such as tricycles and other toys and worse, a toddler.

No Government Action Yet

National Highway Traffic Safety Administration spokesman Tim Hurd acknowledged that backover cases, especially those involving injury or the death of a child, "are very sad and tragic."

Indeed, Fennell said stats show that "in over 60 percent of the cases, it's a parent or close relative who's behind the wheel."

A widely publicized example: Last year, Long Island pediatrician Dr. Greg Gulbransen fatally injured his 2-year-old son, Cameron, in the family driveway. The father had been unaware his toddler son had come out of the house and was at the driveway as Gulbransen backed up his BMW X5 SUV.

While NHTSA officials believe that the more information drivers have about their surroundings the better, the agency isn't looking to mandate reverse park assist systems that now are offered in aftermarket shops and as factory equipment on some vehicles, Hurd said.

Nor is NHTSA interested in adding outside warning beeps to every vehicle as it backs up. "That was studied a number of years ago," he said, adding the study showed a child is apt to be drawn to a beeping vehicle, rather than flee from it. In addition, he said, it's debatable how effective audible beeps would be in a parking garage where a number of vehicles are likely to be backing up at the same time.

Push Is On

Fennell isn't pushing for an audible warning outside vehicles like that found on construction and garbage trucks. She said children can confuse the beeping sound with "an ice cream truck."

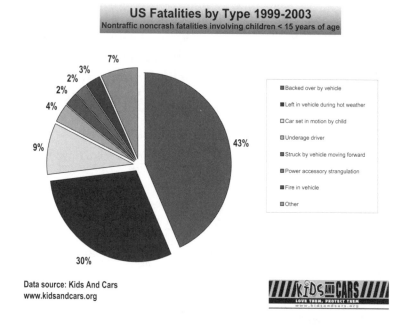

US Fatalities by Type 1999-2003
Nontraffic noncrash fatalities involving children < 15 years of age

- Backed over by vehicle
- Left in vehicle during hot weather
- Car set in motion by child
- Underage driver
- Struck by vehicle moving forward
- Power accessory strangulation
- Fire in vehicle
- Other

43%
30%
9%
4%
2%
2%
3%
7%

Data source: Kids And Cars
www.kidsandcars.org

She is working with the Advocates for Highway and Auto Safety as well as Consumers Union in pushing for a mandate that would make standard some kind of "backover warning and prevention devices" that would alert drivers on all vehicles, including cars, by the 2007 model year.

She also wants insurers to give owners of such vehicles a credit. "The problem is only getting worse," she said.

What To Do Right Now?

Fennell's 1999 Lexus RX 300 didn't come with any backup warning system when she bought it.

So she went to aftermarket shops and had devices installed. One is a rearview video camera from auto supplier Donnelly. Another is an audio system that coaches her with verbal announcements as she backs up to tell her if she's 8 feet away or 6 feet away from an obstacle.

Consumers today can do the same thing, with prices starting under $300. For a quick review of such systems, visit the Specialty Equipment Manufacturers Association.

Increasing Offerings from Automakers

Consumers also can look among today's cars, SUVs, vans and pickup trucks to see which ones offer backup systems right at dealerships.

For example, BMW offers park distance control on even its base X5 SUV now. It operates using ultrasonic sensors in the bumpers, and alerts drivers with beeps heard inside the vehicle. It's a $700 option on the 3.0i and 4.4i and standard on the top-of-the-line 4.6i.

Even entry-level SUVs, like Ford's Escape, now offer reverse sensing systems. In fact, such a system, that also uses ultrasonic sensors, is standard on the top-of-the-line Escape Limited.

Meantime, Toyota's Sienna minivan offers a backup video camera. The camera, which comes standard on vans with the navigation system, works whenever the Sienna is in reverse gear.

A video camera mounted in the tailgate automatically displays a wide-angle view of what's behind the vehicle.

The camera system also is available on the Lexus RX 330.

Meantime, on the Sienna's uplevel XLE Limited model, there's also a new park-assist system that utilizes a sonar range-finding system.

With two front sensors for drive mode and four rear sensors for reverse, the system gives audible beeps—more fast-paced as distance diminishes between the Sienna and a standing object—in order to alert drivers before they hit something.

Automaker engineers note that it's important for drivers to keep these systems—whether camera or sensors—free of dirt so they work properly.

A Parent's Lapse Can Be Fatal
in the Summer Heat

BY JEANNE WRIGHT
LOS ANGELES TIMES, MAY 5, 2004

As summer approaches and temperatures soar across the country, parents and care givers need to be vigilant in preventing heat-related deaths of children trapped or accidentally left in vehicles.

Last year, a record 42 children died nationwide after being left in cars, trucks and vans. Since 1996, more than 200 children have died in this manner across the United States, according to Janette Fennell, president of Kids and Cars, an auto safety advocacy group that has been tracking such incidents.

Many of these tragedies occur when frazzled parents on their way to work or struggling with hectic schedules forget the child is in the vehicle, Fennell says.

Though some find it hard to fathom how a parent could forget a child in a vehicle, Fennell and other child safety advocates say it has happened to the best of parents. "Many of these parents are educated, loving and were devoted to their children."

This year, three children have already perished from being left alone in sweltering cars. Disturbed by the growing number of such deaths, Fennell suspects that simple parent inattentiveness is not the only factor in children being left in vehicles.

She notes that, for safety reasons, many parents place their children in rear-facing seats in the back seat, rather than the front seat, putting children out of sight. And if the child is seated far back in a large SUV, the parent may be even more likely to forget the child.

In 1991, the National Highway Traffic Safety Administration began encouraging parents to put their children in the back seat to prevent them from being injured if the air bags deploy. As a result, the number of air bag injuries involving children has decreased, according to NHTSA spokeswoman Liz Neblet.

But statistics appear to indicate that "we have now lost more children to heat-related deaths than from air bag incidents," Fennell says.

Copyright 2004, *Los Angeles Times*. Reprinted with permission.

Some Tips to Prevent Tragedy

Among experts' suggestions on keeping children safe:

- **Always put something**—cellphone, briefcase, purse—in the back seat that you will need to retrieve when you get out. It will guarantee that you'll open the back door and see your child.
- **Keep a large teddy bear** in the child's car seat when no one's in it. When the child is placed in the car seat, bring the teddy bear up front as a reminder that your child is in the back seat.
- **Warn children** not to play in or around vehicles. Always lock car doors and trunks and keep keys out of children's reach.
- **Keep rear fold-down** seats closed to help prevent children from getting into the trunk from the passenger area of a vehicle.

Even if that's true, Neblet says, the NHTSA still believes the safest place for a child is in the back seat. "We don't want people to be putting them in the front seat just so they remember to pull them out," she says. "If they aren't remembering to take their child out of the back seat, I would not blame it on an air bag."

UC Irvine professor Mark Warschauer's son Michael died last summer when he unintentionally left the sleeping child in his car when he went to work. By all accounts, Warschauer was a devoted parent, and the Orange County district attorney's office determined the incident was an accident.

Since his son's death, Warschauer and his wife, Keiko Hirata, have been active in educating families on how to prevent this kind of tragedy. They have also joined Kids and Cars and other safety advocates in supporting federal legislation to require the NHTSA to collect data on heat-related deaths and encourage the auto industry to acquire technology that would alert parents if a child was left in a vehicle.

"Of course ifs parents' responsibility to take care of their children," says Warschauer, who notes that buzzers and lights alert drivers about seat belt use. "Certainly we could have a safety device to remind you if you left a child in the car."

Fennell says many people don't understand how quickly a closed vehicle can heat up. A recent study by Jan Null, a meteorologist and adjunct professor at San Francisco State, found that the temperature in a car can rise 19 degrees within 10 minutes.

In August, a 2-year-old Ontario girl was treated for heat exhaustion after she was found slouched over in a locked car in Corona. The child had been in the vehicle for only about 15 minutes. The temperature outside was about 100 degrees at the time. A passerby broke a window and rescued the girl while her mother was shopping. Authorities said the temperature inside the car was 122 degrees 10 minutes after the window had been broken.

"Parents and caregivers need to get the word that a car is not a babysitter . . . but it can easily become an oven," Null says.

Children and Air Bags

What's the Problem?

- Most new cars have air bags for front-seat passengers. When used with lap/shoulder belts, air bags work very well to protect older children and adults who ride facing the front of the car.
- Air bags do not work with rear-facing child seats (those used with infants).
- Air bags could seriously injure or even kill an unbuckled child or adult who is sitting too close to the air bag or who is thrown toward the dash during emergency braking.
- In a crash, the air bag inflates very quickly. It could hit anything close to the dashboard with enough force to cause severe injuries or even death. Because the back of a rear-facing child seat sits very close to the dashboard, the seat could be struck with enough force to cause serious, or even fatal injuries to a baby.
- Even older children (who have outgrown child seats) are at risk from a deploying air bag, if they are not properly restrained with a lap/shoulder belt.

What Should I Do?

- The rear seat is the safest place for children of any age to ride.
- An infant in a rear-facing child seat must ride in the back seat if your vehicle has a passenger side air bag (babies under 1 year and 20 pounds should always ride in a rear-facing seat).
- Make sure that everyone in the front seat is properly buckled up and seated as far back from the air bags as is reasonably possible.
- Make sure that all young children are properly secured in a child safety seat and older children by a lap/shoulder belt. Know how to properly install your child seat in the vehicle. Read both the owner's manual for the vehicle and the instructions for your child safety seat.

Where Can I Get More Information?

Call NHTSA's toll-free Auto Safety Hotline at 1.800.424.9393.

Written information and "tip sheets" are available by writing to:

Child Safety Seats
National Highway Traffic Safety Administration
400 7th Street S.W. NTS-1 3
Washington, DC 20590

Source: National Highway Traffic Safety Administration

SUV Capable, But
What About Driver?

By Richard Rubin
Charlotte Observer (North Carolina), February 28, 2004

If you believe the commercials, sport utility vehicles rule the roads, climbing over sidewalks and splashing comfortably through wintry weather.

But plenty of SUVs landed in ditches and snowdrifts this week.

What gives?

Turns out it's the drivers, who often overestimate their vehicles' power.

"There's no doubt that SUVs offer increased traction, but they're not the panacea that many people that drive them think they are," AAA Carolinas spokesman Tom Crosby said.

Only about 5 percent of SUV drivers actually take their cars off-road, Crosby said. In bad conditions, he said, "They don't understand the SUV capability very well or the way their vehicle's going to react."

Four-wheel drive gives drivers better grip on the road, particularly on hills. But, experts say, ice is ice. Once a heavy SUV is moving quickly, it's just as hard to stop as a sedan, said Douglas Love, a spokesman for *Consumer Reports*.

"A lot of times, they think four-wheel drive means they can go faster and do more, but not in stuff like this," said Jamey Green, operations manager at Bradley's Wrecker Service in Charlotte.

Used right, SUVs can help drivers through rough conditions. Leigh Stevens of Charlotte swears by her Honda CR-V, one of the smaller SUVs. On Thursday, she drove carefully and passed other SUVs stuck on the side of the road.

"It's kind of nice to feel a little secure," she said. "I have confidence in that car, even though it's small."

On Friday, her husband, Patrick, a Pineville police sergeant, decided not to take his patrol car to work. He drove the SUV.

Paige Sheehan, a Medic spokeswoman, said paramedics told her some SUV drivers appeared to be a little overconfident on the road. But, she added, a lot of the drivers able to help when ambulances slid off the roadway were in SUVs.

Reprinted with permission of *The Charlotte Observer*. Copyright owned by *The Charlotte Observer*.

A generation ago, nearly all Charlotte drivers might have been flustered by snowy weather. But the country's rapid southern migration is changing that pattern, mixing more patient Northerners with natives who can be overconfident or overly cautious, experts said.

That combination can be dangerous because people move and stop at different speeds, said Wes Brown, a partner in Iceology, a California-based firm that analyzes driving psychology.

"You have a lot more people living in areas where they're either not used to weather they're going to be seeing or they're used to weather they're no longer seeing," he said.

Count Jonathan Gerhard of east Charlotte in the latter category. He grew up in snowy Binghamton, N.Y., and moved here 10 years ago. Gerhard said he maneuvered through Charlotte capably in his Honda Civic on Thursday. He wishes SUV drivers would ease up.

"If I could afford an SUV and the gas and the insurance, I'd love to have [one]," he said. "But it doesn't mean I'd drive like an idiot."

National Survey of Drinking and Driving Attitudes and Behaviors, 2001

By U.S. Department of Transportation, National Highway Traffic Safety Administration
Traffic Tech, June 2003

Since 1991, the National Highway Traffic Safety Administration (NHTSA) has conducted a nationally representative telephone survey every two years to measure the current status of attitudes, knowledge, and behavior of the general driving age public about drinking and driving. These surveys track the nature and scope of the drinking-driving problem (see *TRAFFIC TECHS* 89, 135, 192, 242). The Gallup Organization conducted interviews with a national sample of 6,002 persons age 16 or older in the United States between November 3 and December 23, 2001. The findings suggest that despite the public's continued concern about drinking and driving, progress in a number of key areas has slowed.

Drinking and Driving Behavior

About 22% of the driving age public has driven a motor vehicle within two hours of consuming alcoholic beverages in the past year, about the same as in 1995. Males are more than twice as likely to have driven within two hours of drinking as are females (32% vs. 14%). Adults age 21 to 29 are the most likely to be drinker-drivers (37% males and 20% female) driving within two hours of alcohol consumption.

Drink-drivers made between an estimated 809 million and 1 billion driving trips within two hours of consuming alcohol in the previous year. This is a decrease of about 5% from the 1999 estimate.

On average, the drink-drivers consume 2.6 drinks within the two hours prior to driving. When the amount of alcohol, timing of drinks, and weight and gender of the drinker are taken into consideration, 2.6 drinks relates to an average blood alcohol concentration (BAC) of .03. About 5% are estimated to have a BAC of .08 or higher. This calculated BAC is slightly lower in 2001 than the .04 estimated in 1999, but is similar to 1995 and 1997 estimates. Drinker-drivers under age 21 consume an average of 5.1 drinks prior to driving.

Article by the U.S. Department of Transportation, National Highway Transportation Safety Administration, *Traffic Tech* June 2003.

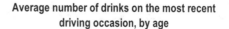

Average number of drinks on the most recent driving occasion, by age

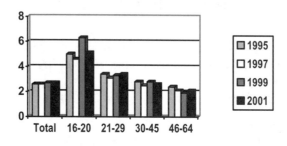

While 16–20 year olds make only about 3% of all drinking-driving trips their BAC levels are nearly three times that of legal age drinkers.

Problem Drinkers

Problem drinkers were defined as having consumed five or more drinks on four or more days in a month, or eight or more drinks on at least one day in a typical month, or who answered yes to two or more CAGE questions (*"Have you felt you should cut down on your drinking? Have people annoyed you by criticizing you about your drinking? Have you felt bad or guilty about your drinking? Have you had a drink first thing in the morning to steady your nerves or get rid of a hangover?"*). Overall, about 11% of the drinking public over age 16 can be classified as problem drinkers. Problem drinkers make up 27% of past year drinking-drivers, accounting for about 46% of all trips in 2001 where driving occurred within 2 hours after drinking. On their most recent drinking-driving trip, problem drinkers were estimated to have a calculated BAC of about .05 compared to .02 for other drinking-drivers.

Attitudes Toward Drinking and Driving

A majority (62%) of persons of driving age believe that they, themselves, should not drive after consuming two or more alcoholic beverages. Nearly all respondents (97%) said that drinking and driving is a threat to their personal safety, which is consistent with past surveys.

Prevention and Intervention of Drinking and Driving

Half of drivers (50%) 16 or older who consume alcoholic beverages report at least one occasion where they refrained from driving when they thought they might have been impaired. This is more prevalent among persons under age 30. Most of these persons rode with another driver (63%).

The proportion of persons age 16-64 who have ridden with someone in the past year who they thought may have had too much alcohol to drive safely has declined significantly from about 15% in 1991 to 12% in 2001.

About one-third (32%) of persons of driving age have been with a friend who may have had too much to drink to drive safely, including half of those under age 30. Most of these (80%) tried to stop the friend from driving and were successful in preventing the impaired person from driving about 75% of the time.

One-third (33%) of those 16 or older have ridden with a designated driver in the past year, with those aged 16-29 most likely (54%), about the same as in the past two surveys. About four in ten drivers (41%) have acted as a designated driver in the past year, consistent with 1999 levels. Designated drivers were reported to have consumed less than one-quarter of one alcoholic drink, on average, prior to driving.

Enforcement

About 1% of the driving age public report being arrested for impaired driving in the past two years. Males under age 30 were most likely to have been arrested (2%). Drinking-drivers are twice as likely, and problem drinkers were four times more likely, to have been arrested for drinking-driving violations.

One-third (33%) of those 16 or older have ridden with a designated driver in the past year.

Most drivers believe that once convicted of impaired driving for a first offense, drivers will receive a fine (46%) and/or a suspended or restricted license (41%). Only 20 percent think the person will go to jail. They generally feel that an impaired driver is more likely to have a crash than to be stopped by police, an increase since 1999. They feel that about 44% will get in a crash while the police will stop about 32%.

Penalties for Impaired Driving

Seven out of ten (71%) feel that drinking-driving penalties should be much (43%) or somewhat more (27%) severe than they are now. Drinking-drivers are much less likely to want penalties to be more severe. About one in three (32%) have seen a sobriety checkpoint in the past year, a significant increase from 1995 and consistent with 1999. About 18% have been through a checkpoint themselves at least once. A majority (62%) feels that sobriety checkpoints should be used more frequently, maintaining support consistent with 1993, but lower than 1995 to 1999.

Blood Alcohol Concentration (BAC) Levels

Over four of five (83%) have heard of blood alcohol concentration levels, but only 27% can correctly identify the legal BAC limit for their state. Those living in .08 BAC states are more likely to correctly know their state's legal limit. More than eight of ten (88%) of those who currently reside in .08 states believe that the limit should remain at .08 or be made stricter, while 53% of those in .10 states feel that their state should lower the limit to .08. About six in ten (61%) feel that all or most drivers would be dangerous at the BAC limit in their state.

Crash Experience

One in six (16%) persons of driving age were involved in a motor vehicle crash as a driver in the past two years. Drinker-drivers (19%) were more likely to have been in a crash than other drivers. Alcohol was involved in about 2% of all reported crashes, and in 4% of crashes by male drivers.

The Zen Commuter

BY JESSIE MILLIGAN
FORT WORTH STAR-TELEGRAM, JULY 22, 2002

Recognize this feeling? It's 5:30 P.M. The world has shrunk to the interior of your car and its relation to a moving and unpleasant mass of chrome bumpers, license plates and brake lights. You aren't even halfway home and your irritability is accelerating faster than the creeping traffic.

One mistake by another driver and you feel your religion may lapse.

This pilgrimage of drudgery is one you make roughly 500 times a year—a common number of trips to and from a workplace.

The number of hours wasted in slow-moving rush-hour traffic is higher in Fort Worth–Dallas than in New York City, Atlanta or Miami, the Texas Transportation Institute reported this summer. A typical Fort Worth–Dallas commuter spent, the institute calculated, about 74 hours idling in heavy traffic in 2000.

That's a staggering length of time spent in states of mind-numbing boredom, road-weary crankiness, or even rage.

Can you make a commute pleasant? Don't count on it.

Can you take the edge off? Yes, if you can find the spiritual side of driving, the Zen in the art of commuting.

America's car culture offers plenty of feel-good stuff massaging seat covers, dashboard aromatherapy diffusers, tip sheets on relaxation exercises, and even wind chimes for therear-view mirror. Everything, it seems, but the plug-in serenity fountain.

Yet experts on driving psychology (and yes, specialists exist) say accessories can help us chill out—but not unless we also get something that money can't buy.

"People may find music or things to calm them, but those things won't be enough by themselves," says Leon James, a professor of traffic psychology at the University of Hawaii in Honolulu, who has studied driver behavior for 25 years. "Your mindset must change."

Accept the fact that long suffering is part of the path of the commuter. Acknowledge that the road is not all yours. Know that every driver, including yourself, makes mistakes, and that these flubs are rarely intentional. Practice forgiveness. Be supportive. Repent, and you are almost home. That's what the experts say.

Article by Jessie Milligan from the *Fort Worth Star-Telegram* July 22, 2002. Copyright © *Forth Worth Star-Telegram*. Reprinted with permission.

"It's amazing how many people get behind the wheel each day and get surprised that there actually is traffic," says Bill Sims, owner of several Sense of Humor Defensive Driving schools in the Metroplex. "They aren't emotionally prepared for this reality, when they should accept that before they even leave the driveway."

Accept that the road will be hard. Then, pray.

"It's helpful to have calming words to say to yourself," says Sims. "When you swear as a result of stimulus, it raises the emotional level, and you end up feeling bad yourself."

Instead of saying "! !!!!@**!" try a mantra of "They must be in a hurry." Or "This, too, shall pass."

"A lot of the things we say or think about other drivers really make us feel worse," says Jerry Deffenbacher, a psychology professor at Colorado State University in Fort Collins. He has studied angry drivers for 20 years.

"Think about things as being humorous," he advises.

When another driver makes a hand gesture, Deffenbacher says to himself: "They are signaling me that I am No. 1."

> **"A lot of the things we say or think about other drivers really make us feel worse."**—
> **Jerry Deffenbacher, Colorado State University,**
> **Fort Collins**

Deffenbacher also is a proponent of accepting our burdens. Bad drivers, detours, slow traffic. We are not being singled out by the universe. All of us run into the rigors of the road.

"It doesn't make sense to insist in our godlike and tyrannical ways that these things are not going to happen to us today." Deffenbacher says.

Contemplate your plight.

"Ask yourself if things are as bad as you think," Deffenbacher advises. "We make things worse by saying to ourselves that things are horrible or catastrophic."

Even lovable smart-alecks Tom and Ray Magliozzi, aka Click and Clack, hosts of National Public Radio's *Car Talk* show, preach kindness.

"Plan to be nice to people during your drive. Commit yourself to making the world a better place," the brothers say on their Web site, *www.cartalk.cars.com.*

Try to react to frustrating situations as if you were walking, not driving, they say. Would you yell at the little old lady who failed to cross the street fast enough?

Don't forget the mind-body connection.

Release stress by taking a few deep breaths, Deffenbacher advises. Lift your shoulders up toward your ears, then drop them. That's about as much car yoga as a driver can take.

Eat proper food, writes Ian Marber in *The Food Doctor in the City: Maximum Health for Urban Living* (Sterling, $19.95). Before driving, cut out caffeine and processed sugar. Maintain steady blood-sugar levels by keeping healthy snacks in the glove compartment. Bags of unsalted nuts are good, he says.

Do not compete with other drivers. Drive the speed limit. Leave your home or workplace a few minutes earlier. Change your work hours if you can. Find a less stressful route home. These are the commands of the driving doctors.

And on top of all that, a little aromatherapy might not hurt.

IV. Insurance and Auto Repair

Editors' Introduction

Even with all the gadgets and gizmos described in the previous chapter, automobile accidents still happen—and often. At that point, drivers must turn to their insurance companies to repair the damage and recoup the losses. They must also find a good garage or auto repair shop when necessary. They hope their insurers can help them with that, too, but before they find themselves in such situations, they must choose the best insurance company for their needs.

Regardless of the boasts made in television commercials, the only way for drivers to find out what auto insurance is best for them is by seeking quotes. Insurance rates vary depending upon not only driving record, miles driven annually, the make and model of the car, and security features, such as car alarms and VIN etching, but also upon factors such as the driver's age, location, and even the color of the car. In her article "Consumer Guide: Auto Insurance" Jocelyn Parker emphasizes the need to shop around for the best deal and suggests that everyone get at least three quotes before settling on a company. "First and foremost," she urges, "you must determine what type of coverage is necessary. Adding certain protections such as collision and comprehensive coverage, which protects a car against fire, theft and vandalism, can add to your costs." Another thing that consumers should recognize is that different states require different types of auto insurance; also, insurance premiums vary greatly from state to state, as the sidebar "States Miles Apart on Auto Insurance" illustrates.

There are even more factors to take into consideration when choosing auto insurance for a teen, according to Lynna Goch in her article, "Gearing Up." Insurers, well aware that the very topic of insurance lacks a "coolness factor," have been trying to build brand identity through tactics such as airing commercials that deal with typically teenage themes such as dating. Despite the fact that some teens do not yet drive and those who do often have parents paying for their insurance, auto insurance companies want to expose teens to their names so that, when the time comes for them to buy their own insurance, they will already be familiar with companies such as Progressive or Allstate. In order to target teens, insurers produce television commercials, launch Web sites, and take out print ads in teen magazines. Some insurers offer added incentives, such as discounts for students who earn good grades.

If, however, an accident should occur, drivers need to have their vehicles repaired. It sounds simple, but deciding on a repair shop proves another problem entirely. In "DRPs: Deciding What's Legal, What's Not," Tina Grady discusses the controversial issue of direct repair program shops, or DRPs. When some drivers report their involvement in accidents to their insurance companies, the companies may refer them to a preferred DRP; however, often customers do not realize that they have options and that they are not required to use the DRPs recommended by insurers. (Though it is not usually mandatory that customers use DRPs for their repairs, some companies do require their policyholders to do so.) Sometimes insurance companies steer their customers by using "word tracks," which entail language suggesting that, if a repair shop is not on the company's DRP, the insurer cannot guarantee the quality or speed of workmanship. In an attempt to support small, independent repair shops, some states have enacted legislation to prevent insurers from directing customers toward DRPs, although other states still allow insurance companies to steer their policyholders. It is a contentious issue, as is the problem of insurance fraud. In August 2002 Democratic Senator Charles Schumer introduced a bill designed to create penalties for those committing auto insurance fraud (see the sidebar "Cheaper Car Insurance Act of 2002"). The proposal is still under consideration.

While insurance companies can help in case of accidents, they can also be a resource in the event of theft. That might be something for owners of 1995 Saturns to keep in mind, for according to John Porretto in "Crooks Like Saturn SL," that vehicle was the most frequently stolen car in 2003. For his article, Poretto interviews those who track trends in auto theft and damage in order to determine why that particular Saturn model, as well as other cars that made the list, are so often targeted.

One last issue that proves problematic for insurers, drivers, and car manufacturers alike is that of recalls due to product defects. As Carolyn Aldred explains in "Brake Applied to Recall Cover," insurance companies have begun to discontinue paying damages on recalls, a policy proving costly for suppliers, as manufacturers increasingly require their component suppliers to bear the risk of recalls. While this is less than an ideal situation for suppliers, it may spawn a positive result, as, since the 2000 and 2001 massive recalls by Ford Motors and Bridgestone/Firestone tires, manufacturers have been focusing their efforts on producing better quality parts.

Consumer Guide: Auto Insurance

BY JOCELYN PARKER
DETROIT FREE PRESS, FEBRUARY 2, 2003

When Heather Johnson began shopping for auto insurance nearly eight months ago, she went to the Internet, where she thought she'd find the least expensive rates for the Oldsmobile Alero she always wanted to buy.

But the 24-year-old Detroit resident was shocked when she got a six-month quote from Geico for $7,000, especially because she didn't have any tickets or accidents on her driving record.

"I went online because they [Geico] always advertise that they are the cheapest, but, in reality, they are the most expensive," said Johnson, who works for the City of Detroit.

Forget what you hear on TV ads. Getting the best auto-insurance rate really boils down to three key things: the type of vehicle you choose, the kind of coverage you need—such as collision or comprehensive—and your shopping techniques. Drivers also might qualify for discounts based on their lifestyle and driving history.

"Shopping around is important. Not all insurance rates are the same," said Frank Fitzgerald, commissioner for the Office of Financial and Insurance Services, which regulates insurance companies in Michigan. "If you're getting quotes that seem high, it shows that you need to do some checking."

Auto insurance rates are based mostly on your driving record, age, where you live, the miles you drive annually, and the make and model of your vehicle.

Michigan buyers have a lot of companies to choose from, including dozens that do business in the state through offices or online. Consumers can use the Internet, an independent agent, the yellow pages or old-fashioned word of mouth to find insurance carriers.

Buyers should get at least three quotes before picking a company, experts say.

These days, getting the best rate is critical because insurance rates are on the rise. Experts say factors such as an increase in insurance fraud and rising jury awards for accident victims will likely drive costs up this year. Drivers, on average, can save more than $1,000 a year simply by shopping around and determining what type of coverage they really need, experts say. Johnson called 11 more agencies and changed the type of vehicle she wanted to buy before choosing State Farm insurance. Now she pays about $2,900 every six months to insure her Chevrolet Malibu.

Article by Jocelyn Parker from the *Detroit Free Press* February 2, 2003. Copyright © *Detroit Free Press*. Reprinted with permission.

"My mom had State Farm, and I dealt directly with her agent," Johnson said. "I got a multivehicle discount because we live in the same house. They also gave me a good driver discount."

First and foremost, you must decide what type of coverage is necessary.

How do you determine what coverage you need?

First and foremost, you must decide what type of coverage is necessary. Adding certain protections such as collision and comprehensive coverage, which protects a car against fire, theft and vandalism, can add to your costs.

There are some types of coverage that are required. Michigan law, for example, says drivers must carry no-fault coverage if they own or lease a car or truck licensed for road use.

No fault includes: personal protection insurance, which pays for personal injury expenses if a driver is hurt in an accident; property damage insurance, which pays for damage done by a driver's car to parked vehicles or fixed properties; and residual liability insurance, which pays when drivers are legally liable for unintentional bodily injury or property damage outside of Michigan.

The cost of a no-fault policy varies depending on the car, your age and how high you set your liability coverage limits. The general rule of thumb is that the more you own—such as a home, boat or other property—the higher your limits should be. This protects you from people going after your assets in case of a serious accident.

Experts recommend carrying only no-fault coverage if a vehicle is worth less than $2,000 because you'll likely pay more for the coverage than you would ever collect on a claim.

You can put the money you are saving by not having more expensive coverage into a bank account. Then you can use the money to pay for damages or a new vehicle in case of an accident. You can literally cut your premium in half by having only a no-fault policy.

If you're buying or leasing a new vehicle, the bank that financed it might require both collision and comprehensive coverage to ensure that the car remains in good condition and that you don't default on payments because you can't make repairs.

Nevertheless, there are ways to keep the costs down. For instance, you can request a higher deductible—the amount a driver pays when an insurance company pays for the rest of the damage—to reduce a premium.

According to Insure.com, increasing a deductible from $200 to $500 on collision coverage can reduce your premium by as much as 30 percent—potentially saving hundreds of dollars.

Finally, you have to decide whether you want all the extras, such as electronic equipment coverage, car-rental coverage and uninsured-underinsured motorists coverage. All those can add to your cost.

States Miles Apart on Auto Insurance

STATE LEGISLATURES, DECEMBER 2003

New Jersey drivers paid the highest average auto insurance premiums in 2001 for the seventh time in eight years, according to the latest report from the National Association of Insurance Commissioners.

On the low end is Iowa where drivers paid barely more than half the average premiums of New Jersey motorists.

Average premiums combine three separate coverages—liability, collision and comprehensive. Because liability coverage is tied to at-fault accidents, the most expensive premiums are in states with the most traffic. The states with the most traveled roads tend to have the most expensive liability coverage. The notable exception is Michigan ($294), with its unique no-fault system that bans most lawsuits in exchange for unlimited medical coverage for people hurt in accidents. The national liability average was $413.

Some of what Michigan drivers save in liability, however, they pay out in collision coverage. With unlimited medical coverage, Michigan paid the most ($416). The national average for collision was $271.

Comprehensive tends to be the cheapest coverage—costing less that $100 in Hawaii and Ohio. However, where auto thefts and hail damage are prevalent, premiums can go above $200. The District of Columbia ($230) tops that list. The national average was $133.

Even with the highest cost in the nation, New Jersey saw its average premium decline 6 percent from 1996 to 2001 while the national average grew by nearly 5 percent. Only two other states saw premium drops during this period—California (10 percent) and Hawaii (25 percent). Eight years ago, Hawaii was in New Jersey's shoes with the highest premiums in the country.

This year, New Jersey passed major reforms to make its highly regulated insurance market more competitive. Like Hawaii, it hopes to leave its national distinction behind soon.

Auto Insurance Coverage

- Liability (required in all but a few states) pays bodily injury and property damage expenses—including legal bills—caused to others in an at-fault accident.
- Collision pays vehicle repair of the person who causes an accident.
- Comprehensive pays for other damages, such as theft, fire, vandalism, natural disasters and even hitting a deer.

Reprinted with permission from *State Legislatures* December 2003. Copyright © National Conference of State Legislatures 2003.

Experts recommend that consumers, especially those in the Detroit area, consider adding uninsured-underinsured coverage, which will reimburse a driver if he or she is hit by an uninsured or hit-and-run driver.

"Underinsured motorist coverage is extremely inexpensive," says Tim Ford, an independent insurance agent and president of Modern Insurance Agency. "It costs about $20 every six months."

About 40 percent of the vehicles in Detroit are uninsured, so it's important to include that coverage, Ford said.

Rental-car insurance could also come in handy because your car could be in the body shop for a month or so for accident repairs. Still, expect it to add $40–$50 to your six-month premium. You could get a rental free or pay a small fee depending on the plan you choose.

When discussing a policy with an agent, always ask about discounts. You can get breaks for things like having a good driving record, driving only a few miles per day, having an anti-theft system in your vehicle and belonging to groups such as Sam's Club, AARP or a college alumni association. Drivers can get 18 percent to 20 percent off their premiums just for belonging to some groups, Ford said.

When you belong to a group "it's perceived that you are a more conscientious person in society and that you are more involved in you community," he said.

Just because you bought a Honda Civic instead of a sport-utility vehicle doesn't mean you'll save much on auto insurance. That's why it's important to consider insurance before you buy a vehicle.

For instance, the Honda Civic Coupe was among the 10 most expensive vehicles to insure last year because of its high theft rate, Insure.com says. Civics are stolen more than other vehicles because their parts carry a high street value, and that drives insurance premiums up. The Mitsubishi Montero Sport, a midsize sport-utility, topped the list of the most expensive vehicles to insure in 2002 because it had the highest number of claims for injury collision and theft.

Drivers under 24 might want to look at something less flashy because they already have their age working against them, experts say. Among the least costly vehicles to insure in 2002 were the Buick LaSabre and Century and the Oldsmobile Bravada.

"My problem is the 20-year-old who wants to drive a 2003 Mustang 5.0," Ford said.

Web sites such as Insure.com provide lists of the vehicles that are the cheapest and most expensive to insure. Insure.com also lists the safest vehicles in 2002, which could help lower your insurance rates.

Gearing Up

By Lynna Goch
Best's Review, October 2003

Teen-age drivers evoke images of reckless speed and its consequences—but insurers see them in a different light. With their
numbers expected to create a babyboom-like demographic bulge by
2010, insurers are busily reaching out to this group. Many auto
writers are starting a dialogue with teens by conducting safety programs and offering discounts on rates not only to encourage safer
driving habits but also to establish their brand in this demographic. For example, the second-largest auto writer, Allstate
Corp., offers full-time students meeting certain grade requirements its "Good Student Discount." Progressive Corp., the
third-largest private passenger writer, is going a step farther and
actively marketing to the 14-to-24 year-old age group with commercials and print advertising linked to the stuff of teen angst—
dating, zits and clothes.

Like their baby boomer parents, Generation Y can't be ignored,
due to their sheer numbers. Currently, there are about 72 million
young people born between 1977 and 1994. And by 2010, there will
be more teens in the United States than ever before, according to
Michael Wood, a teen expert and vice president of marketing
research firm Teenage Research Unlimited. This boomlet means
teens will be the majority of the adult population for the next two
decades, which will be a rich marketing vein for insurers to tap.

Teen experts caution, however: Don't ignore this age group or use
the same old messages to try to reach them. "The prime directive is
you can't market to them. As soon as you market to them, whatever you are selling is no longer cool," said Peter Shankman, chief
executive officer of The Geek Factory, a New York City–based teen
marketing and public relations firm. Shankman said it's important
to lock them into an insurance brand as soon as possible. "Grab
them early and they will be yours for life. Insurance has no coolness factor like jeans. You'll never see a report that Tom Cruise
switched to Geico and that's cool. There is no socially accepted
stigma to make them change," Shankman said.

Even though a teen might not be buying auto insurance by her-
self now, she's forming impressions about the brand today, Wood
said. "When it's time to build the relationship with an insurer, they
are bringing with them any perceptions about the brand—both
positive and negative," Wood said.

Article by Lynna Goch from *Best's Review* October 2003. Copyright © A. M. Best Company.
Reprinted with permission.

Getting to Know You

Generation Y, like teens before them, have distinct characteristics. Because most are the product of two-income families, teens have a great deal of disposable income. With teens spending $170 billion in 2002, their disposable income is at an all-time high, and that figure doesn't include spending by parents that's influenced by the teen, said Wood.

Teens today also are very optimistic and are used to good economic times. They have a dramatic impact on their parents' spending as well, giving input on consumer selections, such as vacation destinations, cars and high-tech items. Wood says this purchasing input stems from their parents' raising them with choices. "So, do you want the cheeseburger or chicken nugget Happy Meal?' they were asked. Now teens have an opinion about products, advertising and marketing and they like to be heard," Wood said.

The Internet remains the biggest differentiator for this generation, however. The Internet is the primary medium of choice for this generation of teens, surpassing television, according to a market research program conducted by Harris Interactive and Teenage Research Unlimited on behalf of Yahoo! Inc. and Carat North America. The study reveals teens are able to multitask in a world of media choices, such as 200-plus cable television networks, 5,500 consumer magazine titles, 10,500 radio stations and 30 million-plus Web sites. The study reveals that Generation Y is a revolutionary consumer group entrenched in the media experience and these patterns will influence the future of media spending. "Marketers have been using the same media strategies since television became the primary medium for most market segments in the 1950s. It's time to rethink," said Wenda Harris Millard, chief sales officer of Yahoo!.

Targeting the Teen

Progressive began augmenting its marketing direction to focus on teens in 2000. At that time, Glenn Renwick, current president and CEO, said the company was setting its sights on teens as customers of the future. "When charged with running a company, you have to know what our customers are going to look like in the next four to five years," Renwick said. "You must take into account what societal changes have occurred. Today's 14-year-old's life revolves around the computer—online chat rooms and research for school. You have to expect how they will react with financial services companies," he said.

Although Progressive declined to be interviewed for this article, it did pass on information about its teen marketing program.

Progressive's reason for reaching out to teens is linked to its goal to become consumers' No. 1 choice for auto insurance. The auto insurer launched its teen advertising campaign in February, calling it "an investment that will pay off in the future." Although Progressive's research discovered only a small percentage of teens actually buy auto insurance themselves, it wants teens to get to know the company so that when it comes time to buy a policy they'll already know about Progressive. "Progressive is an innovator, and we believe that this is the first-ever auto insurance ad campaign exclusively targeting teens," Progressive said.

Clothes and dating—typical teen issues—are the themes of the print ads. Pro-

> *Only a small percentage of teens actually buy auto insurance themselves.*

gressive said the ads were designed to talk to teens in their own language and familiarize them with the concept of insurance in ways that they would find useful in their lives. Progressive said the ads also convey a message to teens that Progressive is one insurance company that will help to de-mystify auto insurance and can offer an easy-to-use policy when they need one. The ads contain Progressive's teen-only Web site address—*teen.progressive.com*, where young consumers can learn how auto insurance works and get information about driving and driving safety.

Since teens spend more time online than any other leisure-time activity, it's important to offer a strong Web presence, said Wood. "There's an educational opportunity here. Teens have questions about buying and insuring a car. There are also a lot of myths out there about insurance," Wood said.

Progressive's teen Web site's art is styled like its print ads, and the site offers "Insurance 101" that tells teens about rates, how to get a quote and how to make the decision whether to get their own policy or stay on their parents' coverage.

In Progressive's teen-targeted print ad campaign, one of the ads shows a female student arriving late for class and discovering she and her teacher are wearing the same outfit. The ad, entitled "Fashion Crisis Insurance," says, "We wish we could insure you against everything from outfit collisions to no refunds. But for now, we can just offer really simple car insurance. When you need some, think Progressive." Another ad even offers a sweepstakes with the chance of winning a date with Los Angeles–based rock band Maroon 5.

Teen expert Wood said "hats off" to Progressive for having a presence in teen media and for embracing this age group and seeing them as an opportunity and not a burden. Wood said Progressive's print ad could be improved, however, simply because teens are so bombarded with marketing messages that "it takes a noteworthy ad to stop and get their attention." The Geek Factory's Shankman said the ads are "very sharp," but also warned Progressive to be careful "not to screw it up" by making insurance seem cool. "It's more important to focus on what will happen if you don't have insurance that will make you uncool," he said.

Progressive's print ads appear in magazines not known to contain insurance advertising—*YM*, *Seventeen*, *Vibe* and *Transworld Skateboarding*.

The insurer's television commercials are designed to help familiarize teens with insurance in ways that they would find useful in their own lives. In the TV spot called "Backyard," teens are attempting to overcome a boring day by using a makeshift catapult to launch various items, ranging from a tricycle to one of the teens. The commercial says, "Clearly these teens need boredom insurance." In another, entitled "Cute Guy," a young girl makes eye contact with a male teen and then trips over a trash can. The commercial adds that's a moment for "social disaster insurance."

The teen-focused television commercials air on MTV, Cartoon Network, ABC Family and Much Music. In the company's second-quarter 2003 earnings conference call, Renwick reported Progressive will direct advertising to college-age and college-type candidates and continue some of its teen advertising.

In 2001, teens accounted for 14% of all motor vehicle fatalities, according to the National Highway Traffic Safety Administration.

It Takes a Village

The statistics surrounding teen driving are hair-raising. In 2001, teens accounted for 14% of all motor vehicle fatalities, according to the National Highway Traffic Safety Administration. Injuries from car crashes are the leading health problem for teens 13 to 19 years old. The Insurance Institute for Highway Safety reports 16-year-old drivers have the highest percentage of crashes involving speeding and caused by driver error.

Some insurers, including Farmers, State Farm and Liberty Mutual, are taking a different tack—addressing parents' concern about teen driving safety. Since most teens learn about auto insurance through their parents and are covered under the family policy, many auto writers are working on creating safer drivers, while offering lower rates, through youth-targeted driver safety programs. These programs help to develop better drivers through the incentive of lower rates.

Safety education programs are an excellent way for auto writers to create good will as well as better risks, said Ray George, director of Prophet, a brand strategy consulting firm. "By educating teens, you are creating a great public benefit and bringing customers on board who are smart and savvy about risk," George said. "Making people smarter can make you stand out in the crowd," George said.

State Farm's "Steer Clear" program, now available in 39 states, has already shown that participants have fewer claims, said Dick Luedke, a State Farm spokesman. It was introduced to encourage young drivers to develop road-worthy habits and because State Farm, the nation's largest auto writer, "values its younger customers and sees them as an important part of the market," Luedke said.

Drivers are eligible for the "Steer Clear" program if they are a licensed driver under 25, have no at-fault accidents or moving violations in the past three years and have all cars in the family insured with State Farm.

The program is completed under the watchful eye of a State Farm agent who provides the video, driving log and magazine *Rearview* to the young driver. Within 60 days of receiving the program, the applicant must watch the video, read the magazine, take a quiz and record 20 to 30 trips in a driving log. The magazine is a graphically catchy publication offering young people an interview with the Grim Reaper, articles on how to drive in dangerous conditions and the Wheel of Misfortune, which shows the consequences of an auto accident. Luedke said young drivers can enjoy up to a 15% discount on their auto coverage after meeting the program's criteria. Currently 20,000 drivers are receiving discounts through the "Steer Clear" program.

Boston-based Liberty Mutual extends its corporate mission to help people lead safer, more secure lives into its teen market segment. "We value long-term relationships with customers, and teens begin a relationship under their parents' policy. Our programs with SADD speak of our commitment to the family," said Alan Schlosberg, vice president and manager, personal marketing, for Liberty Mutual. The eighth-largest private-passenger auto writer has had an 11-year relationship with Students Against Destructive Decisions, including its 4-year-old Teens Today project.

Liberty Mutual's original teen-safety program—"Avoiding Collisions"—contains activities to help teens recognize the consequences of excessive speed, the dangers of night driving and the importance of seat belts. The program is advertised through television commercials and is also marketed through the company's customer newsletter. To date, more than 4 million people have viewed the video, said Schlosberg.

Liberty Mutual wanted to do more to promote teen driving safety, so four years ago, together with SADD, it began conducting research on various teen behaviors to help parents with typical teen issues of drinking and driving, communicating and what parents can do to improve the reality gap that exists between them and their children.

Given its strong research findings, Liberty Mutual hopes parents will respond to the results and act on them. For instance, in its 2002 study looking at how teens make decisions, Liberty Mutual found that between sixth and seventh grades there is a huge spike in using alcohol and drugs and it jumps even more among ninth-graders. The study also reveals, however, that teens who have an open communication with their parents are more likely to live up to their parents' expectations.

Liberty Mutual sees its association with SADD as the example of its approach to the teen driving market—by focusing on safety.

The fourth-largest private passenger auto writer—Los Angeles-based Farmers Insurance Group—sees its role as the valuable third party in getting the message of safety to teens. Ten years ago Farmers introduced its "You're Essential to Safety" program, but revamped it in 2000. "We did focus group research and learned [that] to reach out to teens we had to have an edgier creative content that the MTV generation can relate to," said Kevin E. Kelso, president of Farmers personal lines.

The "Wrecked" program was born out of the focus group research and features a reality-based video with actual stories of teen drivers talking about the consequences accidents have had on their lives, including death, permanent injury and prison time. "The video is painful to watch, much more powerful than standing in front of flip charts. We also use the work book to drive home the points to young drivers about issues they never thought about," Kelso said. "Wrecked" allows parents and teen drivers to discuss the issues together and also provides a driving agreement that makes the teen commit to the privilege of driving. Farmers reports accident frequency is 10% to 15% less among participants in the "Wrecked" program. Out of Farmers 400,000 teen drivers, about 65% participate in the program, Kelso said. Farmers is taking another step in its safety mission by piloting a bumper sticker program in northern California. The bumper sticker idea is modeled after the signs seen on heavy rigs across the United States that read, "How's My Driving?" and includes an 800 phone number to call with reports. The idea of the "I Saw You" program is to understand what happens when a teen goes out, and the insurer helps the parent, Kelso said.

While Farmers' safety programs demonstrate a marketing benefit, it remains focused on safety. "We're trying to do something helpful. What's important is to teach young drivers how to be safe," Kelso said.

DRPs: Deciding What's Legal, What's Not

By Tina Grady
Automotive Body Repair News, January 2002

When a customer gets into an accident, his or her first priority is usually to call the insurance company, then take the vehicle to a collision repair shop. Sometimes the customer already knows where he or she wants to take the car because of previous work done or because of a recommendation. But then there are those customers who don't have a repair facility in mind. This provides the insurance company with the opportunity to "strongly recommend" a collision repair shop to that customer-to influence a customer, and in a sense, "steer" him or her to one of the insurance company's preferred direct repair program (DRP) shops. Many times, they aren't required to disclose that the customer has the right to choose a repair facility. Some states don't have this type of legislation in place.

Additionally, some insurance companies use "word tracks." These include language insinuating that if a shop that is not on an insurer's DRP is used, the quality of the work and how quickly it will get done cannot be guaranteed. But how do you determine if this is steering or just an insurance company trying to ensure the best repair job for its policyholder?

Laws Vary State by State

It's difficult to determine what's legal and what's over the line because anti-steering legislation varies by state. In North Carolina, for example, the state ratified House Bill (HB) 13 in October to incorporate penalties for insurers who steer customers and to make the language clearer that this type of practice is not only frowned upon—but illegal. The bill, originally developed to clarify that motorists are not required to use shops which are part of insurer DRPs, underwent several revisions even before it was ratified. The bill further enforces existing anti-steering legislation in North Carolina, specifying that insurers may not recommend any shop without also telling the consumer he or she is under no obligation to use that shop. It also establishes penalties for violations.

Reprinted with permission from *Automotive Body Repair News*, January 2002, pages 46–48. *Automotive Body Repair News* is a copyrighted publication of Advanstar Communications Inc. All rights reserved.

As the bill was originally written, it was left to the insurance commissioner's discretion about how to notify insured that they are able to choose any repair facility.

The ratified version does not require a separate notice, but it specifies that disclosure be added to the policies. This portion of the bill becomes effective April 1 and applies to policies issued or renewed on and after that date.

However, the real challenge comes with ensuring that the legislation is enforced. Like North Carolina, most states have laws prohibiting insurers from requiring a customer to go to one of their preferred facilities. But there are ways for them to get around what would "technically" be construed as steering. Word tracks that promise lifetime warranties and higher quality, more efficient work and easier claims handling, many times "steer," though not directly, customers to insurers' preferred shops.

DRPs have often been compared to health maintenance organizations (HMOs) because they are tightly managed and some are restrictive.

A Collision Repair HMO?

DRPs have often been compared to health maintenance organizations (HMOs) because they are tightly managed and some are restrictive. HMOs are managed through a primary care physician, who serves as a "gatekeeper" to the patient before he or she is able to see any other doctor, and the HMO decides whether it will cover particular operations. Similarly, some insurer DRPs require concessions and discounts-despite the denial of this by many insurers. This blurs the line between what's legal and what's not.

In states such as Alabama and Alaska, customers may choose their own repair facility. However, neither of these states prohibit insurance companies from requir-ing repairs to be done in specific facilities and there are no regulations that require them to inform customers of their right to choose.

Mike Carpenter, a painter at Tony Carpenter's Body Shop in Morristown, Tenn., has faced challenges in his state because Tennessee does not prohibit DRPs, and it doesn't prohibit insurance companies from requiring repairs to be done in specific facilities. The state also does not have disclosure regulations.

If repairers don't let customers know they have a choice, then insureds are left in the dark and many collision repair facilities are left without work. "We've been in business for 20 years, but here we are with no work," Carpenter says. "It's just too hard for independents not on a DRP list to compete."

If a customer is handed a list with three or four shops on it, Carpenter says, he or she is likely to go to one of those shops. "If a customer says, 'I want to take my car to Mike or Tony Carpenter,' and the insurer says, 'You can take it there, but it's not on our list and we don't stand behind that work,' the customer is more likely to go with a body shop the insurer is touting, Carpenter says. It's not like we don't know what we're doing," he adds. "How [a shop] gets work is sometimes a joke."

Insurer-Owned DRPs

The Allstate acquisition of Sterling and Progressive Insurance Co.'s pilot version of "Concierge" (a working title, not an official designation) is raising even bigger concerns for what's legal and what's not. Progressive Insurance Co. launched its pilot program in at least four cities, including Bedford, Ohio; Orlando, Fla.; Philadelphia; and Richmond, Va., that offers 'an end-to-end' claims-handling service for customers, an approach that would essentially eliminate repair shops' direct contact with customers. (See "Insurer plan clips shop-to-customer contact," *ABRN News,* August 2001.) On May 8, Allstate also announced that it had bought the Sterling Collision Centers consolidator chain from a group of private investors.

Sharon Merwin, collision division director for the Automotive Service Association (ASA), says the Sterling acquisition and Progressive's program brings to the table the issues of where you draw the line between the insurance company having a vested interest in the industry versus a controlling interest. "There's a difference between insurers making financial contributions to the industry and them taking a controlling interest," she says.

But it's incredibly difficult to decipher exactly where the line should be drawn, she says. If an insurer owns a body shop, such as Allstate owning the 39 Sterling facilities, it doesn't necessarily mean there is steering going on, Merwin says. However, just thinking logically, Allstate or another insurer is almost invariably going to encourage that an insured get his or her vehicle repaired at the insurer-owned shop. So although steering may not have actually taken place, "If you think a customer will go to someone else's shop, you're crazy," Merwin says. What's more, she says, is that a program such as Progressive's "Concierge" almost promotes steering. Since it eliminates the customer contact with the shop, repairers aren't given the chance to build relationships with customers. This "removes the checks and balances" of the system, Merwin says, and "if you remove the checks and balances, how can you check anything?" However, Merwin says she is sure that customers will raise concerns with programs such as these. Not all customers are savvy when it comes to the collision repair process, but here are some very picky owners, Merwin says. To them, their vehicle is one of their most important, and most likely, second most expensive possessions, so they want to know where their cars are and who is repairing them. "Some [owners] will say, 'I want control over my possessions,'" she says. "I'm not so sure customers want to have their rights taken away."

Retaining Control

Chris Dameron, safety standards manager for True2Form Collision Centers in Raleigh, N.C., and member of ASA has been a long-time anti-steering advocate and has been outspoken about the issue. Like Merwin, he says that Progressive's program also heightens his concerns about steering. "I have a problem with it because Progressive takes complete control of the process," he says.

This cuts out the repairer-customer contact, which in turn, eliminates the repairer's opportunity to build a relationship with a customer-or with an insurance agent for that matter. This makes it easier, he says, for steering to occur, because an agent can no longer refer a customer and the customer wouldn't know which shop to take his or her vehicle to, anyway. This helps ensure that the insurer is able to send the policyholder to the shop it wants the vehicle to go to. "I wouldn't be surprised if this is [legally] pushing the envelope on steering," Dameron says. Similarly, Allstate's mandate in several states, including Pennsylvania and Minnesota, that

---

"It's tough to determine some of the situations and whether steering has taken place because we don't know what's being said between the consumer and insurer."—
Chris Dameron, True2Form Collision Centers

---

agents may no longer direct work to a particular shop—as in a referral because of a relationship, not because of steering—is also crossing the line as to whether steering is taken place. The claims department is now directing where cars should go. But it's always to a company-owned PRO or PRO 2000 shop, not independents. "There is no question there is some steering going on," Dameron says.

Providing Proof

He adds that once steering occurs, it's very difficult to prove or to do anything about it. He says it's also hard to determine when steering has taken place. For example, if a vehicle comes to your shop and then it's moved, you can logically assume either the customer is not pleased with the shop or steering is taking place. But the only things a shop owner can do are go to a customer and confirm suspicions, Dameron says. But to do this, it's essential to have a good relationship with the customer—which is why the "Concierge" program is disturbing to many repairers. "Building a relationship with a customer is essential to determining steering," he says. "It's not hard to determine what steering is. It's tough to determine some of the situations and whether steering has taken place because we don't know what's being said between the consumer and insurer." That is unless a customer specifically informs a shop owner about an insurer's coercive actions. If you suspect an insurer is steering work away from your facility or if you find out from a customer that he or she was being persuaded to use a particular facility, then you need to take it up with the insurer, Dameron says. If a vehicle is moved from your facility and then you ask a customer why and he or she explains that it was at the suggestion of the insurance company, then you need to ask the insurer for an explanation. "Tell the insurer you spoke with the customer and you are wondering why work is being taken away from your repair facility," Dameron says. However, he cautions, an antagonistic approach is not always the best choice.

DRPs Are Not the Source of All Problems

Although many repairers see steering and DRPs as going hand in hand, that doesn't mean these insurer referral programs are the source of all problems for independent repairers. "True2Form has some DRPs," Dameron says. "There's nothing wrong with recommending shops. And there is nothing wrong with DRPs." In fact, in

---

Shops may just live with the insurer's steering practices because they don't want to deal with the time and expense necessary for a lawsuit.

---

some areas, if a shop is not part of a DRP, such as in the Washington, D.C., metro area and in small towns, it may be hard to make ends meet, he says. The problem comes in when insurers strong-arm customers and shop owners. "DRPs take a lot away from free enterprise," Dameron says. "You run into the question, 'Where is the freedom of choice going?'"

There's always the threat of having to take legal action, but shops may just live with the insurer's steering practices because they don't want to deal with the time and expense necessary for a lawsuit.

However, some shops, such as Pack Brothers Paint and Body Shop in North Carolina, have filed lawsuits. The North Carolina shop filed *Pack Brothers Paint and Body Shop Inc. and Ronnie Pack vs. Nationwide Mutual Insurance Co. (a.k.a. Nationwide Insurance Enterprise) and Joe Benkendorf* last February in an attempt to stop the insurer's practices and keep the shop from losing money.

Pack Brothers attributes "a substantial loss in revenue of several thousand dollars" to what the shop says are steering practices by Nationwide. Ronnie Pack, who owns the shop with brothers Larry and Victor, says Nationwide's actions have financially hurt the business Pack says, but this case is about more than money. It's about stopping large insurance companies from controlling body shops and from acting only in the best interest of the insurers, he says. "This is being done to a lot of little guys," Pack told ABRN after the lawsuit was filed. "And then [the insurers] get big body shops and use them to promote their programs. They use them to control rates."

Some shop owners believe that you should always litigate if there is a question of steering, but be aware that it costs both the shop owner and insurer a lot of time and money and nullifies any semblance of a relationship that both parties may have with one another.

"You cannot look at things coldly and say, 'This is illegal,'" says Bob Redding, Washington, D.C., representative for ASA and legal expert on collision industry issues.

It's just not that cut and dry, he says.

Dameron adds that the only way that steering will ever truly be eliminated would simply be to, "get rid of DRPs."

Cheaper Car Insurance Act of 2002

(Introduced in the United States Senate)

To create a penalty for automobile insurance fraud, and for other purposes.

IN THE SENATE OF THE UNITED STATES

August 1, 2002

Mr. Charles Schumer introduced the following bill; which was read twice and referred to the Committee on the Judiciary

A BILL

To create a penalty for automobile insurance fraud, and for other purposes. Be it enacted by the Senate and House of Representatives of the United States of America in Congress assembled, SECTION 1. SHORT TITLE. This Act may be cited as the "Cheaper Car Insurance Act of 2002." SEC. 2. AUTOMOBILE INSURANCE FRAUD.

(a) IN GENERAL—Chapter 47 of title 18, United States Code, is amended by inserting at the end the following: "Sec. 1037. Automobile insurance fraud" (a) Whoever knowingly commits automobile insurance fraud shall be punished as provided in subsection (b). (b) Except as provided in subsection (c), the punishment for an offense under subsection (a) is a fine of not more than $100,000 and imprisonment of not more than—

1. 5 years for a first violation of subsection (a);

2. 10 years for a second violation of subsection (a); or

3. 15 years for a third or subsequent violation of subsection (a). (c) If a violation of subsection (a) results in costs that exceed $100,000, the fine imposed under subsection (b) may be in an amount greater than $100,000 in order to cover the resulting cost. (d) In this section—

   1. the term "automobile insurance fraud" means fraud committed by any person who knowingly and intentionally presents a written statement, causes a written statement to be presented, or prepares a written statement with knowledge or belief that it will be presented to or by an insurer, self-insurer, or any agent thereof, that such person knows—

      (A) contains materially false information concerning any fact material to an application, certificate, evidence, or claim referred to in paragraph (2); or

      (B) conceals, for the purpose of misleading, information concerning any fact material to an application, certificate, evidence, or claim referred to in paragraph (2); and

   2. the term "written statement" means a written statement that is part of, or in support of—

      (A) an application for the issuance of or the rating of a commercial insurance policy;

      (B) a certificate or evidence of self-insurance for commercial insurance or commercial self-insurance; or

      (C) a claim for payment or other benefit pursuant to an insurance policy or self-insurance program for commercial or personal insurance. (b) CONFORMING AMENDMENT—The chapter analysis for chapter 47 of title 18, United States Code, is amended by adding at the end the following:

      "1037. Automobile insurance fraud." SEC. 3. BEST PRACTICES. (a) IN GENERAL—The Department of Justice shall publish best practices for the States to use—

1. in licensing auto body shops that perform work paid for by insurers; and
2. in licensing medical treatment provided to people who are injured in automobile accidents. (b) GOAL—The goal of publishing best practices as required under subsection (a) is to encourage the States to adopt such practices to limit the feasibility of committing insurance fraud. SEC. 4. INVESTIGATION OF FRAUDULENT PRACTICES. (a) IN GENERAL—The Attorney General shall cooperate with the offices of the United States Attorneys to—

1. aggressively investigate fraudulent chop shops and salvage yards;
2. aggressively prosecute automobile insurance fraud (as defined in section 1037 of title 18, United States Code); and
3. report statistics on investigations, prosecutions, and convictions of automobile insurance fraud. (b) REPORTING—Statistics referred to in subsection (a)(3) shall be reported to the Subcommittee on Administrative Oversight and the Courts of the Committee on the Judiciary of the Senate and the appropriate Committee of the House of Representatives. SEC. 5. INVESTIGATIVE AND PROSECUTORIAL SPECIAL UNITS. (a) ESTABLISHMENT OF UNITS—The Attorney General shall establish investigative and prosecutorial special units in the offices of the United States Attorneys in the 10 cities in the United States that are most severely affected, as determined by the Attorney General, by automobile insurance fraud (as defined in section 1037 of title 18, United States Code). (b) PURPOSE—The special units established under subsection (a) shall investigate and prosecute automobile insurance fraud.

Crooks Like Saturn SL; Asian Cars Closing In

By John Porretto
Newsday, June 6, 2004

The 1995 Saturn SL was the nation's most-stolen vehicle last year based on thefts versus the number of models registered, but hot-selling cars from Asian manufacturers remain popular targets and big sport utility vehicles are gaining ground, a recent report shows.

One out of every 200 registered 1995 Saturn SLs was stolen in 2003, placing it ahead of the 1998 Acura Integra and the 1994 Saturn SL as the vehicle thieves targeted most, according to Chicago-based CCC Information Services Inc., an insurance industry tracker of trends in theft and vehicle damage.

CCC changed the way it calculated its list for 2003, combining stolen-vehicle data with vehicle registrations from R. L. Polk & Co. to determine the rate of theft as a percentage of registered models. It had reported only the brand and model year of those vehicles pilfered the most in a calendar year.

Toyota Camry and Honda Accord, two of the best-selling vehicles in North America, fell from the top of the list to the middle of the top 25. Acura, Honda's luxury brand, had six versions of the Integra in the top 10.

"We can't determine the exact reason thieves prefer some vehicles, but our data suggests some cars are stolen for the value of their parts, which may explain why we often see a 'clustering' effect with [specific] models from sequential model years," said Mary Jo Prigge, CCC's president of sales and service. "Some manufacturers retain the same part-type from model year to model year, so a part from a 1993 model may fit a car manufactured three years later," Prigge said.

CCC, which provides software and information services to insurers and repair shops, receives loss claims from more than 350 property and casualty insurers in North America. The annual report is based on total losses for vehicles that are stolen and not recovered, or stripped to the point of being a total loss.

CCC spokeswoman Jeanene O'Brien said the shift to using theft and vehicle registration information provides more detail to the industry and consumers.

Reprinted with permission of The Associated Press.

"It's simply a more comprehensive snapshot of vehicle theft," she said. "You're not only looking at what was stolen but what was available to steal." Vehicles from the mid- to late-1990s were the most intriguing to thieves, CCC said. Vehicles made in 1997 were most susceptible, followed by model years 1996, 1995, 1994 and 1998.

Saturn spokeswoman Sue Holmgren said the brand, a division of General Motors Corp., had no internal data showing high theft rates, but she noted the automaker has made significant changes to its ignition system since 1995. One enhancement disables the vehicle's fuel supply if it's started without a key.

Honda spokesman Chuck Schifsky said, "It's important to make sure we continue to put the latest immobilization technology into vehicles. But when you're dealing with popular vehicles, they're going to be ones that tend to be stolen."

The average age of a stolen vehicle last year was 6.64 years, the study shows. Acura was the nameplate with the most stolen models, followed by Suzuki, Honda, Mitsubishi and Infiniti. And Chevrolet Suburban, Cadillac Escalade and GMC Yukon are becoming more popular theft targets, CCC said.

Brake Applied to Recall Cover

By Carolyn Aldred
Business Insurance, April 5, 2004

As automobile manufacturers increasingly require their component suppliers to bear the risk of recalls due to product defects,
many suppliers are carrying this massive exposure without insurance.

Product recall insurance for the automotive component sector has
grown scarce in recent months following American International
Group Inc.'s decision to withdraw from this line of coverage. Brokers say AIG was the leader in this market for U.S. risks.

Manufacturers are paying more attention to this exposure in the
wake of the massive uninsured recalls in 2000 and 2001 by the
Ford Motor Co. and Bridgestone/Firestone Inc. of defective tires on
Ford vehicles.

Auto parts manufacturers and their brokers now are beating a
path to the London and Bermuda markets to try to find alternative
capacity for product recall insurance. Already some underwriters
are starting to step into the void left by AIG's departure, but only
on a limited basis.

"During the last five years, vehicle manufacturers increasingly
have demanded that suppliers cover the costs of recalls caused by
faulty components. Component companies are speaking to us
about recall insurance. They feel they are being squeezed by the
manufacturers and cannot afford to buy recall insurance," said
Melanie Wiseman, senior legal advisor for the London-based Society of Motor Manufacturers & Traders Ltd., a trade group.

U.S. component manufacturer Delphi Corp. stated in its annual
report that product recall is becoming a more significant risk for
suppliers because "vehicle manufacturers are increasingly looking
to their suppliers for contribution when faced with recalls."

A Growing Concern

Although most auto component companies and manufacturers
would not discuss the issue of product recalls in detail, they agreed
the challenge of insuring this risk is causing growing concern in
the industry.

Reprinted with permission from *Business Insurance*. Issue of April 5, 2004, copyright 2004.
Crain Communications Inc. All rights reserved.

The risk manager for a German auto manufacturer, who did not wish to be named, acknowledged that the costs associated with an automotive recalls can be substantial, creating a huge business risk for suppliers that, "given their financial standing, need some protection."

> *"A recall . . . can feasibly run into many millions of dollars."*—A risk manager

A risk manager for a U.S. auto component supplier, who also did not wish to be named, said that product recall insurance capacity for parts suppliers is "virtually nonexistent." His company had a small amount of very limited coverage under a special extended products liability policy, as part of its general liability coverage, but AIG this year refused to provide any umbrella coverage above the policy.

"Insurers do not seem prepared, since Ford/Firestone, to provide coverage at any price," he said, noting that his company is increasing efforts to ensure quality to minimize the risk of defective products. The risk manager said he is considering setting up a captive insurance company to cover its risk.

"There is a need and a desire to secure recall cover, but U.S. insurers are not offering it so auto component companies are looking to Bermuda and London," said the risk manager for another U.S. auto component supplier.

"A recall can cost many times the selling price of the component involved and can feasibly run into many millions of dollars," said another risk manager. "Thankfully, quality practices have risen to meet the challenge so far, but the potential for the 'big one' is always out there with the potential to bring down the whole company," he said, adding that product recall "is the one risk that has the potential to keep me awake at night."

David Lacey, director of risk and insurance for Troy, Mich.-based ArvinMeritor Inc., agreed that a lot of car manufacturers, particularly ones based in Europe, ask suppliers to buy product recall insurance to cover their exposure. However, it is a product that has always been very expensive and often provides only low limits, he said, noting that ArvinMeritor does not buy it.

"It is a business risk we chose to self-insure," he said.

Seeking Alternatives

In recent months, brokers have been working hard trying to find markets to replace AIG on product recall programs. AIG was the largest single market for U.S. auto component suppliers, offering up to $15 million of broad product recall coverage per policyholder through its WorldSource Crisis Management Division, brokers say.

AIG confirmed that "it has reduced its presence in the automotive product recall arena" but would not comment on the reasons for this move. An AIG spokesman noted that its New York-based World-

Source division continues to offer product recall insurance for other industry sectors, including food and beverages, sporting goods and apparel.

The withdrawal of AIG from this line starting last year caught the market by surprise and left brokers and underwriters unprepared to offer alternatives, noted Justin Whitehead, director of Lloyd's of London broker R. K. Harrison Insurance Brokers Ltd.

R. K. Harrison, broker for one of London's leading product recall insurance lineslips for the food and beverage industry, has been trying to find alternative markets for U.S. auto component manufacturers, said Mr. Whitehead.

Although London is one of the leading markets for insuring product recall/product contamination risks, most underwriters typically concentrate on the food and beverage sector and on first-party product recall risks, he noted.

"Most auto suppliers want third-party coverage to cover the costs of a recall by their automaker customers. The London market is being quite slow to come to grips with this broader coverage," explained Mr. Whitehead, noting, however, that there are "very limited pockets of capacity."

Syndicate 2003, managed by Catlin Underwriting Agencies Ltd., and two other Lloyd's syndicates are jointly providing up to $5 million of capacity for automotive component manufacturers "on a very selective basis," said a Catlin spokesman.

"Underwriters are being very selective and only insuring manufacturers with revenues up to $500,000," he said, pointing out that the availability was "layer-based" and would probably mean large retentions and possible gaps in some layers for policyholders.

New Markets

Several leading product recall/contamination underwriters in London are now considering "opportunities" in the automotive industry.

Jennie Seabrook, underwriting manager-crisis management for QBE International Insurance Ltd., confirmed that the insurer is offering recall coverage to small to midsize automotive suppliers for noncritical component parts on a worldwide basis, including the United States. Such components include panels, plastic moldings, stereos and carpets, she said.

"The drivers for this type of coverage are suppliers who are being placed under pressure to produce evidence of a recall policy, in order to fulfill their contractual obligations to supply," said Ms. Seabrook.

QBE's coverage is on a first-party basis only, covering the risk of recall following accidents, tampering or design defects that harm property owned by a third party, Ms. Seabrook explained.

The coverage covers such recall expenses as the cost to destroy and replace recalled products, consultant costs, loss of gross profits for up to 12 months and a expenses, subject to a sublimit, for rehabilitation of the product's image and reputation, she said.

Tina Kirby, product recall underwriter for Lloyd's syndicate 623/2623, managed by Beazley Group P.L.C., also is studying automotive product recall risks.

"There is a huge gap in the market for automotive manufacturing suppliers and it is an area we are looking at, but it is a completely different sector from food and beverages and we need more information," she said.

European Outlook

U.S. component companies are struggling more than their European counterparts to find coverage.

U.S. component companies are struggling more than their European counterparts to find coverage, partly because AIG dominated the U.S. product recall market for the automotive sector, said Ian Harrison, director of Miller Insurance Services Ltd.

Also, European insurers, particularly German insurers that have close and long-term relationships with their industrial policyholders, often provide limited product recall insurance through their general product liability programs, said Mr. Harrison.

"The issue is more acute for small to medium-sized manufacturers who need low retentions" and are not bringing large umbrella product liability programs to the market, he said.

But the increasing costs of automotive recalls also are forcing some German insurers out of the product recall market, said Patrick Nuhn, a specialist automotive product recall underwriter with Hanover, Germany based HDI Industrie Versicherung A.G.

HDI still offers recall insurance contracts for German and other European auto component suppliers as an extension of their public and products liability programs, he said. Under certain circumstances, this may cover U.S. subsidiaries of German or European companies, he added. HDI, however, does not provide cover for U.S. auto component manufacturers without a European parent, Mr. Nuhn said.

The number of auto recalls has increased significantly since 1997 for several reasons, according to Mr. Nuhn. He said these include:

* Shorter development time for new models.
* Complex new technologies in new cars.
* An increase in the quantity of electronic components in cars.
* An increasing number of vehicle models built on the same or similar platforms, using the same or similar components.

- More development activities and responsibility being shifted to component suppliers from carmakers.

Rob Best, a partner of London-based broker JLT Risk Solutions Ltd., said that European automotive component manufacturers typically can get third-party product recall coverage through financial or economic loss extensions bought as part of their general product liability programs.

Mr. Best also noted that several Bermuda-based insurers offer third-party recall coverage through excess-layer product liability programs.

However, that type of coverage is only available at a high level and not always suitable for small manufacturers, he added.

Craig D. Simon, managing director of Willis' Casualty Marketing Practice in New York, said that it is the smaller to mid-sized automotive companies that are having most difficulty obtaining coverage for recall risks because "the standard U.S. markets have stopped writing this business."

"There are creative solutions in the marketplace to help the larger manufacturers fund for this risk," he noted.

"There is such a thing as secondary product recall coverage for automobile component manufacturers in the German market, though the insurance industry has grown very wary and restrictive about offering it," said Steven Bechofer, manager in the corporate risk management department of Munich-based Infineon Technologies A.G.

"It is not unusual that this coverage is coupled with high, multi-million euro deductibles, restrictive limits and in-depth, extensive risk assessments," he said.

R. K. Harrison's Mr. Whitehead said that few underwriters are willing to extend product liability policies to cover recall risks, though some Bermuda excess liability insurers and Swiss Reinsurance Co. are more willing to consider it.

Marcus Schulze, vp of corporate risk underwriting for Swiss Re in Zurich, confirmed that Swiss Re will provide product recall insurance for automotive industry manufacturers with revenues in excess of $1 billion with a minimum attachment of $25 million.

V. The Auto Industry: A
Global Perspective

World Motor Vehicle Production, 1950-2002

Year	United States	Canada	W. Europe	Japan	Other	World Total	U.S. % of World Total
1950	8,006	388	1,991	32	160	10,577	75.7
1960	7,905	398	6,837	482	866	16,488	47.9
1970	8,284	1,160	13,049	5,289	1,637	29,419	28.2
1980	8,010	1,324	15,496	11,043	2,692	38,565	20.8
1985	11,653	1,933	16,113	12,271	2,939	44,909	25.9
1990	9,783	1,928	18,866	13,487	4,496	48,554	20.1
1991	8,811	1,888	17,804	13,245	5,180	46,928	18.8
1992	9,729	1,961	17,628	12,499	6,269	48,088	20.2
1993	10,898	2,246	15,208	11,228	7,205	46,785	23.3
1994	12,263	2,321	16,195	10,554	8,167	49,500	24.8
1995	11,985	2,408	17,045	10,196	8,349	49,983	24
1996	11,799	2,397	17,550	10,346	9,241	51,332	23
1997	12,119	2,571	17,773	10,975	10,024	53,463	22.7
1998	12,047	2,568	16,332	10,050	12,844	53,841	22.4
1999	13,107	3.042	17,603	9,985	14,050	57,787	22.7
2000	12,832	2,952	17,678	10,145	16,098	59,704	21.5
2001	11,518	2,535	17,825	9,777	16,170	57,705	19.7
2002	12,328	2,624	17,419	10,240	16,975	59,587	20.7

Note: Data for 1998-2001 may not be fully comparable with earlier years because derived from different source.

Source: American Automobile Manufacturers Assn.; for 1998-2000: Automotive News Data Center and Marketing Systems GmbH

From *World Almanac & Book of Facts 2004*. Copyright © *World Almanac & Book of Facts*. Reprinted with permission.

Editors' Introduction

The first car manufacturers were Frenchmen Panard and Levassor (1889) and Peugeot (1891). The first automobile to be mass-produced in the United States was the 1901 Curved Dash Oldsmobile, built by car manufacturer Ransome Eli Olds. By 1913 Henry Ford introduced automated conveyer belts to the assembly line for the production of his Model T, and car production really took off. Since then, the car markets in the United States and Europe have boomed, but, bit by bit, vehicle production has moved into Asia. In just over five decades, car production in Japan alone has increased over 300 percent (see the chart entitled "World Motor Vehicle Production, 1950–2002").

In an unusual turn of events, larger numbers of supposedly foreign cars are now being made in the United States. Jim Fuquay reports in the article "Foreign Cars Aren't Quite So Foreign These Days" that car plants owned by foreign companies such as Toyota and Honda are increasingly common in the U.S. In 2002, for example, Toyota celebrated its 10 millionth vehicle built in North America, where they have been manufacturing cars for over 16 years; the company has factories in the United States, Canada, and Mexico. Volkswagen's Pennsylvania factory, which began operations in 1978, was the first foreign brand to open in the United States. That foreign companies would choose to open plants in North America is logical, however unexpected; the United States is the world's largest car market, with annual vehicle sales topping 17 million in 2000 and 2001.

In the area of car production, it seems that Asian companies are not only encroaching upon North America but are leading sales in Europe, too. In his article "Smug No More," Jerry Flint explains, "For years the American auto industry suffered and the Europeans were a bit smug. They were hot, they were profitable, they built prestige cars. . . . Suddenly, sales of Japanese and Korean vehicles are climbing fast in Europe while local makers stand still." Whereas sales of European autos from brands such as Volkswagen, Daimler-Chrysler, and Peugeot dipped and companies like Renault and BMW stayed level, Toyota's sales are up 24 percent, Mazda's 33 percent, Honda's 19 percent, and Korean companies Hyundai and Kia 17 percent. With European car manufacturers losing sales, Flint ponders what course of action they will take.

Meanwhile, it seems that Charles J. Murray has nothing but praise for Japanese design and implementation in his article "Japan's Design Practices Get Credit for Its Reliable Cars." He cites a recent survey of vehicle reliability as conducted by Consumers Union, which suggests that Asian-manufactured cars exceed both North American and European models in system reliability. While China is not known for its auto production abilities, the Chinese have recently begun to embrace the car, which Clay Chandler documents in "China Goes Car Crazy." In 2002 sales of passenger cars exceeded 1 million for the first time ever. By the following year, one out of every 100 Chinese owned a car, a figure which, although still significantly fewer than one out of every two Americans, represents a major increase in vehicle ownership in China. Some individuals are not as concerned about car production close to home, but about energy production.

One issue that has plagued American drivers for decades is the United States' reliance on foreign oil, and, since the beginning of the U.S.-led wars in Afghanistan and Iraq, Americans' ties to Middle Eastern oil look shakier than ever. Gasoline prices have soared and consumers are looking for alternate sources of energy. Unsurprisingly, oil and alternate fuels have also become an issue in the 2004 presidential campaigns, as Robert Collier points out in "Oil Erupts as Issue in Presidential Campaign." Senator John Kerry has pledged to "work for a real energy policy for this country that decreases America's dependence on foreign oil and helps lower the costs to American families." Likewise, President George W. Bush has said, "We need to produce [energy sources] in our own country, and we need to encourage exploration in our own hemisphere so we're less dependent on other parts of the world." These statements are not unfamiliar; even in the1970s, President Richard Nixon promised to find alternatives to Arab oil. However, at this stage in the current presidential campaign, neither candidate has proposed any viable options for decreasing the country's reliance on imported oil.

Foreign Cars Aren't Quite So Foreign These Days

By Jim Fuquay
Akron Beacon Journal, September 1, 2002

When Toyota rolled out a new red Camry at its Tennessee assembly plant in July, it marked both a milestone for the Japanese company and a trend in U.S. manufacturing.

It was Toyota's 10 millionth vehicle built in North America, including factories in the United States, Canada and Mexico. And it highlighted the growing percentage of "foreign" cars that are now "Made in the U.S.A."

It has been 16 years since Japan's biggest automaker started building cars in the United States—and 24 years since Volkswagen's Pennsylvania factory became the first foreign brand to build in the heart of the world's biggest car market.

In that time, the Big Three U.S. automakers—General Motors, Ford and Chrysler—have seen their share of the U.S. market erode. But the percentage of autos built in North America has risen slightly. That's because foreign automakers have steadily increased their production in North America, investing tens of billions of dollars and hiring tens of thousands of American workers.

Toyota, for example, built more than 500,000 vehicles in North America last year—69 percent of what it sold in the United States. Honda leads all foreign nameplates with 76 percent.

"It surprises people. When they hear the word Toyota, they think 'made in Japan,'" said Jim Wiseman, a Toyota vice president at the company's North American headquarters in Georgetown, Ky.

Consider another wrinkle in global car building.

GM's Saturn brand agreed in July to buy 50,000 engines a year from Honda. But instead of boosting the foreign content of the Saturn Vue, the move will make Saturn cars more American. That's because the Honda engines will be built in Ohio, while the engines Saturn previously used came from Britain.

Honda, which built its 10 millionth North American vehicle in 2001, says it has invested more than $7 billion in North American production facilities.

Copyright 2002 UPI. All rights reserved. This article reprinted with permission. RsiCopyright Clearance License # 3.5955.1870383-37735.

The Association of International Automobile Manufacturers, a trade group that includes big automakers from around the world, estimates that its members have plowed about $25 billion into U.S. plants and equipment. The group said those operations employ more than 70,000 people and buy more than $26 billion in parts.

The trend isn't confined to the United States. For example, Toyota expects to sell 40,000 Australian-made Camrys in the Middle East next year.

But with annual vehicle sales topping 17 million each of the past two years, North America is at the center of manufacturers' attention.

"There's an awful lot of automotive investment in North America. It just isn't by the same old companies," said Mike Wall, auto analyst at IRN Inc., a consultant in Grand Rapids, Mich.

The Honda-Saturn engine deal also illustrates another significant trend, Wall said.

When the Japanese manufacturers started assembling cars in North America, many parts were imported or supplied by companies with close ties to the manufacturers.

"There's an awful lot of automotive investment in North America. It just isn't by the same old companies."—Mike Wall, auto analyst, IRN Inc.

"Domestic content didn't use to be significant," Wall said. "But that is on the increase. Nissan, Honda and Toyota have significant engine operations in North America."

The activity by foreign manufacturers in North America approaches the frenetic. Consider:

- In June, Nissan said it will spend $500 million to expand its Canton, Miss., plant by 1 million square feet, boosting capacity by another 150,000 vehicles. Nissan only broke ground on the plant in April 2001. The expansion is expected to boost annual capacity to 400,000.

- Honda opened its Lincoln, Ala., plant ahead of schedule last November to meet demand for its Odyssey minivan. In July, it announced a $425 million expansion that will boost capacity to 300,000 vehicles a year by 2004. Honda is also expanding its Ohio engine plant capacity to nearly 1.2 million a year.

- In April, Hyundai broke ground on its Montgomery, Ala., assembly plant, the South Korean automaker's first in the United States. Ohio Gov. Bob Taft tried to entice Hyundai officials to build the plant in Ohio, but failed after officials spent more than $21,000 on the effort.

The plant is expected to be able to produce 300,000 vehicles a year and employ nearly 2,000 people.

Although millions of vehicles continue to stream into the United States from overseas, the export market works both ways.

Mercedes-Benz, for example, last year built about 80,000 of its M-Class sport utility vehicles at its Tuscaloosa, Ala., plant. About 35,000 of those were exported.

Toshiaki Taguchi, chief executive of Toyota Motor North America, recently told Automotive News that "10 years from now, my hope is that North America will become a base for developing unique models that we could export to other parts of the world." The automaker has the capacity to build 1.1 million vehicles in North America, most of which goes to satisfy the U.S. market.

In July, Toyota's 50/50 joint venture with GM, California's New United Motor Manufacturing, started exporting the Pontiac Vibe/Toyota Matrix that it builds at the plant.

It will sell in Japan as the Toyota Voltz.

Smug No More

By Jerry Flint
Forbes, May 10, 2004

Everybody gets a turn in the box. For years the American auto industry suffered and the Europeans were a bit smug. They were hot, they were profitable, they built prestige cars, and even the Asians couldn't push them off the road.

Suddenly, sales of Japanese and Korean vehicles are climbing fast in Europe while local makers stand still. That's not all. The dollar is shrinking against the strong euro and eroding the huge profits that were coming from America.

Costs and quality issues that didn't seem important in the past are becoming serious. And even the basic strategies of European car companies are being called into question.

Europe isn't yet the U.S., where foreign nameplates take 51% of the car sales (a few of those names, such as Volvo and Saab, are Detroit-owned) and 25% of the truck sales.

In Europe the Japanese for years took about 10% of the business and the Korean share was minuscule. Those shares began growing last year. In two months this year the Japanese had 13% of the sales and the Koreans 4%, or a combined 17%.

Look at it another way. In the first two months of this year native European companies Volkswagen, Peugeot, DaimlerChrysler and General Motors (Opel) were down 6% in sales from the year-before two months. The Ford group is down 1%, and Renault and BMW are even (thanks to a gain for BMW's little Mini). Fiat is up nearly 3%.

But Toyota's sales in Europe are up 24%, Mazda's up 33%, Honda's up 19%, and sales of the Korean firms Hyundai and Kia up 17%.

Why are the Asians so hot? Some industry leaders talk about the currency advantage they get from the strong euro—since in euro terms their Japanese yen and Korean won prices are low. But I think that more-important reasons are new models, more variety, long-standing quality reputations and improved diesel engines.

One more thing: In Europe the Asians do poorly in the countries that are home to auto companies but extremely well in smaller countries that don't make cars. Toyota got 3% of the market in Germany and France and 5% in Italy last year. But Toyota won 16% of the market in Norway and Ireland and 15% in Finland. Hyundai and Kia had 2% in Germany and 1% in France but 4% in Norway

Reprinted by Permission of *Forbes* Magazine © 2004 Forbes Inc.

and Ireland. As car sales climb in the eastern European states that are joining the EU, my guess is that Asian cars will get a disproportionate share there, too.

The Japanese both build in and export to Europe. Toyota, Nissan and Honda build in Great Britain, but all the Asians are spreading out. Toyota built a plant in France, and some Asian firms are going to eastern Europe, where the labor is cheap.

The euro is a serious problem because of the profits the German companies (not the French or Italian Fiat) made in the U.S. "Even with hedging, the fall in the value of the dollar is cutting into the earnings of every German auto company," writes auto analyst Maryann Keller. If the euro stays at $1.26 or higher, it's bad news. "German car companies can raise prices, sell fewer cars and see their profits collapse, or they can hold the line on prices and see their margins shrink," she says.

The currency change unmasks a more basic issue: high labor costs—they love that 35-hour week over there—and low productivity. Quality is another problem: Mercedes and VW, particularly, have tarred their reputations.

The Europeans, even more than Americans, hate to close factories and lay off workers.

Then there are strategic questions. VW is moving up the income scale with expensive cars and acquired luxury nameplates, while the new VW Golf, the bread-and-butter car, is not setting Europe afire. That's trouble.

Daimler's global dream is a nightmare. Mitsubishi, which it controls, is a disaster, and Chrysler is fighting to get out of the red while doubts are raised about Mercedes' quality.

Opel and Ford have been losing money in Europe. They have switched from American to European leaders, which should help, but the market is getting tough.

Europeans might have been able to handle many of these problems if it weren't for the Asians' growth. The Europeans, even more than Americans, hate to close factories and lay off workers. Politicians don't like it, and neither do the workers. They riot and burn tires.

So what will the Europeans do? Go with incentives (as Detroit is doing) and give away the profits? Find some sneaky way of protection? Import from China? Restructure? Squeeze the partsmakers? Boost productivity and quality? Or just lose the business, as Detroit did?

We'll see what they learned from Detroit's mistakes.

Japan's Design Practices Get Credit for Its Reliable Cars

By Charles J. Murray
Electronic Engineering Times, March 22, 2004

Japanese design philosophies are responsible for the superior electrical and electronic reliability of Asian-made automobiles, automotive experts said after the Consumers Union released its latest vehicle-reliability survey earlier this month.

The results of the owners' survey, published in the April issue of *Consumer Reports* magazine, suggest that Asian-made autos exceed North American models and are far superior to the European luxury cars in system reliability. Three Japanese nameplates—Acura, Infiniti, and Lexus—made the list of vehicles with the most reliable electrical and electronic systems. Three German nameplates—Audi, BMW, and Mercedes-Benz—ranked among the least reliable.

The philosophical difference that leads to such disparities is that "the heart and soul of the Japanese philosophy is the system, rather than the individual component. That's the opposite of the philosophy of American and German automakers," said David Cole, chairman of the Center of Automotive Research (Ann Arbor, Mich.), which did not take part in the study. "European and American manufacturers have a history of believing that perfect parts make perfect systems."

Even so, the problem may be less the parts themselves than the design and assembly processes that knit them together—a factor that would appear to favor a holistic design approach. When electronic systems fail, it's often not the fault of the microcontrollers, memories, or other ICs, the Consumers Union and others said. Indeed, microprocessors have become exceptionally robust in recent years, according to the Consumers Union (Yonkers, N.Y.).

Rather, the source of problems is often traced back to the use of connectors in assembly. "We find a very high correlation between reliability and the number of connections made at the assembly plant," Cole said.

Some dashboard assemblies, he noted, have as many as 45 connections that need to be made in the factory; others have as few as three or four. It's no leap to conclude that the ones with more connections are more likely to be incorrectly assembled, and in fact that's the case, Cole said.

Copyright © 2004 by CMP Media LLC, 600 Community Drive, Manhasset, NY 11030, USA. Reprinted from *EETimes* with permission.

Japanese manufacturers have dominated the *Consumer Reports* system-reliability surveys because "they make an effort to develop a foolproof system, making sure the wires don't rub against sharp pieces of metal and connections go together with an audible snap, so that the line worker knows the connection has been made," said David Champion, director of testing at Consumers Union's automotive test facility (East Haddam, Conn.).

Cole of the Center of Automotive Research added that Japanese manufacturers have benefited from a slightly slower adoption rate for cutting-edge electronics, whereas competitors in the United States and particularly in Germany have been more aggressive in their adoption of high-tech features. "Through the school of hard knocks, the Japanese manufacturers have learned that sometimes it's better to be a littler slower," he said.

Experts noted that the reliability struggles of European manufacturers are not new. For the past two decades, they said, reliability has been on the decline among European carmakers, while reliability has risen slightly in North America and dramatically in Japan.

Much as their American counterparts did in the 1970s, however, European automakers have proved slow to institute the changes needed to improve reliability.

"The European carmakers for some time have made the assumption that they own the quality game, always have and always will," Cole said, "But the data has shown repeatedly that's not true anymore."

> *Reliability has risen slightly in North America and dramatically in Japan.*

Survey Details

Consumers Union engineers said that the Japanese Lexus and German BMW were found to be at opposite ends of the reliability spectrum not only in electronics but across the board—engines, transmissions, suspensions, exhaust, brakes, and other areas. Based on surveys from approximately 675,000 respondents, they found that eight-year-old Lexus LS400s had fewer problems per hundred vehicles (41 per 100) than six-month-old BMW 7 Series vehicles (42 per 100).

According to *Consumer Reports*, the Lexus LS430 is currently priced at approximately $55,000, while the BMW 7 Series sells for $69,000 to $117,000.

Vehicles cited in the study for poor electrical and electronic reliability include the Audi A6, BMW 7 Series, Chevrolet Blazer, Ford Windstar, Mercedes-Benz E-Class, Volvo 850, and Volkswagen Golf, among others. Consistently offering the best electrical and electronic reliability were the Acura Integra, Honda CR-V, Infiniti QX4, and Lexus LS400.

Teardown Lessons

Consumers Union engineers said their experience in tearing down vehicles tells them that the causes of electrical and electronic malfunctions run the gamut from improperly installed wiring to bad connectors to faulty relays. Such problems can manifest themselves in the breakdown of all manner of automotive components, including window motors, starters, alternators, batteries, gauges, wipers, lights, air bags, fuel pumps, and water pumps.

But Champion rejected the idea that more electronics results in more electronic problems, arguing that sufficient statistics exist to refute that claim. "Lexus, Acura, and Infiniti have produced vehicles with more features and greater complexity, yet they seem to get it right."

Consumers Union engineers did acknowledge, however, that electrical and electronics still tend to be larger problem areas than more established technologies, such as body integrity or body hardware.

China Goes Car Crazy

BY CLAY CHANDLER
FORTUNE, AUGUST 11, 2003

In late April, as authorities in Beijing mobilized to contain the SARS virus, 33-year-old Li Yang climbed into her red Suzuki Alto and headed west. Slipping out of the city hours ahead of a government quarantine, she "just kept going, to see how far I could get." Six days and 1,600 miles later, she arrived in Lhasa, the Tibetan capital. Thrilled and exhausted, she posted a notice on the Internet, documenting her adventure with digital photos and appealing for a companion to share the drive home.

For centuries such freedom of movement has been unimaginable in China. In feudal times, poverty, bad roads, and imperial edict confined subjects of the Middle Kingdom to the villages where they were born. Mao kept the masses close to home by banning private car ownership and imposing a rigid household registration system. Now all that is changing. After nearly a quarter century of economic liberalization, car ownership is suddenly within reach of millions of ordinary Chinese. As incomes rise, new car prices plummet, and the government adds new roadways, China's 1.3 billion inhabitants are eager to trade their bicycles for a faster set of wheels. In 2002 passenger car sales topped one million for the first time. In the first six months of this year, China's new car sales surged 85% over the same period last year.

Foreign manufacturers are flocking to China to claim a stake in the fast-growing market. Volkswagen, China's biggest foreign automaker, has promised to invest $6.8 billion over the next five years to increase capacity. General Motors, which has spent $1.5 billion to build a state-of-the-art factory in Shanghai, also has bold plans. Japanese giants Toyota, Nissan, and Honda have all established joint ventures with Chinese partners. And the boom has just begun. Only one in 100 Chinese owns a car, compared with one in two Americans. But in the richest Chinese cities—Shanghai, Beijing, Guangzhou—annual incomes are approaching $4,000, the level at which private-car consumption shifts into high gear.

The profusion of cars has launched a new cultural revolution, transforming Chinese life and society in ways that bear surprising resemblance to what happened in America 50 years ago. The most obvious change is the traffic. Beijing's broad boulevards are now choked with cars at rush hour. In Shanghai the bridges and tunnels crossing the Huangpu River are so congested that a cab ride

Article by Clay Chandler from *Fortune* August 11, 2003. Copyright © 2003 Time Inc. All rights reserved.

from one side to the other can be an hour long ordeal. To prevent gridlock, the Shanghai city government auctions a limited number of new car license plates each month. Over the past two years the city has increased the number of plates on the block to 3,000 a month from 500, but demand has soared, driving the minimum successful bid to more than $4,000. Even with these restrictions, the number of gas-guzzling vehicles on Chinese roads is multiplying so fast it poses a grave threat to the environment and could reshape the global economics of oil.

Beijing now boasts drive-in movie theaters. Prospering yuppie SUV owners band together for off-road excursions to the Great Wall. Some have organized weekend drag races. The newsstands display a riot of motor magazines, where readers can ogle domestic and import models. Private-car ownership has spawned a new class of commuters, too, who motor to downtown office towers from spacious, modern homes in the suburbs. "I enjoy the drive," says Zhu Wen, manager for a Dutch food additives company, of the 30-minute trip to his office in central Shanghai. Zhu lives with his wife and infant son in a gated community with a familiar name: Long Island. The grounds are immaculately landscaped, and the homes come in French, Italian, and English Tudor models. "It would probably be cheaper to ride a taxi every day," Zhu confides. "But this way I have more freedom."

Li Yang can attest to the appeal of the open road. Her Internet posting failed to find anyone to share the drive back. But it captured the imagination of hundreds of Beijingers trapped in the city: On the journey home, her mobile phone was deluged with text messages from nearly 1,000 vicarious fellow travelers wishing her godspeed.

Oil Erupts as Issue in
Presidential Campaign

By Robert Collier
San Francisco Chronicle, April 20, 2004

With gasoline prices at all-time highs and expected to surge further in the coming months, it's no surprise that Sen. John Kerry and President Bush are drawing their campaign battle lines over how to fix America's dependence on costly foreign oil.

But there is little indication that the debate shaping up will give relief at the pump—or any change in U.S. reliance on imported oil—any time in the foreseeable future.

Americans are continuing to shift from smaller, more fuel-efficient cars to gas-guzzling giants, the disconnect between campaign rhetoric and reality is growing, and analysts say the long-term implications for U.S. foreign policy are virtually unexamined.

Ever since President Richard Nixon boldly pledged to wean the nation from imported oil after the Arab oil boycott in the early 1970s, every president has made the same promises. And every one has failed miserably to deliver. The 2004 election is unlikely to change that trend.

Instead, the experts say, the United States is almost guaranteed to become increasingly dependent on the Middle East—and especially Saudi Arabia—for decades to come. Despite its much-criticized links to terrorism, Saudi Arabia is likely to maintain its privileged position as the uncomfortable ally that the United States can't do without.

Terrorism, war in the Middle East and oil are making for a potent mix on the campaign trail.

On Monday, Kerry pounced on a report that Saudi Arabia's ambassador to the United States has promised Bush the Saudis would boost oil output this summer to reduce prices and help Bush win the November election. White House spokesman Scott McClellan declined to deny the report, thus boosting Kerry's charges of a "a secret White House deal" that had artificially rigged oil prices.

Kerry signaled that he plans to use his pro-conservation agenda on the campaign trail, saying, "Unlike George Bush and his friends at the big oil companies, I'm going to work for a real energy policy for this country that decreases America's dependence on foreign oil and helps lower the costs to American families."

Republished with permission of *The San Francisco Chronicle* from "Oil Erupts as Issue in Presidential Campaign," by Robert Collier, April 20, 2004; permission conveyed through Copyright Clearance Center, Inc.

In recent weeks, Kerry has made similar promises. "Our young men and women will never have to fight and die for foreign oil," he said March 30. He added that he would "create 500,000 jobs in renewable energy and building the vehicles of the future," and promised that "America will be energy independent from Mideast oil in 10 years."

But Kerry gave no details about how he would do any of this, and the administration has put him on the defensive by counterattacking.

A Bush TV ad that has run repeatedly in recent weeks notes that Kerry supported a 50-cent-per-gallon tax in 1994 as part of a plan to reduce the federal deficit. The ads say the measure would have cost the average U.S. family $657 per year.

"Energy independence" is impossible any time soon, no matter which candidate wins in November.

"Some people have wacky ideas, like taxing gasoline more so people will drive less. That's John Kerry. He supported a 50-cent gas tax," an announcer says in the commercial. "Raising taxes is a habit of Kerry's—he supported raising gasoline taxes 11 times. Maybe John Kerry just doesn't understand what his ideas mean to the rest of us."

Kerry seemed to backpedal, insisting that he would not raise gas taxes. He then dug up a proposal in the 1980s by Vice President Dick Cheney, then a Wyoming congressman, for a $5-per-barrel tax on imported oil.

Since 2001, the Bush administration has tried to coax Congress to pass a comprehensive energy bill designed by a task force headed by Cheney. Congress again rejected the bill in November.

"We need more energy production close to home," Bush said in an October speech advocating the bill. "We need to produce in our own country, and we need to encourage exploration in our own hemisphere so we're less dependent on other parts of the world. Our nation and our hemisphere have got natural gas. . . . But this resource has been hampered by restrictions on exploration."

Bush, however, has not spoken on the issue in recent months. Analysts say his silence may be an attempt to defuse Democrats' attempts to portray him as beholden to Big Oil.

Analysts say that "energy independence" is impossible any time soon, no matter which candidate wins in November. Reasons include:

Saudi dominance. During Bush's 2000 election campaign, he criticized the Clinton administration for allowing the Organization of Petroleum Exporting Countries to dictate the world's oil prices, and he promised to "jawbone" OPEC to lower them. Despite the new report of a U.S.-Saudi deal, some observers say it is unlikely.

World Oil by the Numbers

World crude oil production—Millions of barrels per day (top 10), 2003

Russia	8.49
Saudi Arabia	8.48
U.S.	7.92
Iran	3.79
Mexico	3.79
China	3.41
Norway	3.25
U.K.	.28
Venezuela	2.01
Iraq	1.33

Proven oil reserves—Billions of barrels (top 10), end of 2001

Saudi Arabia	261.8
Iraq	112.5
UAE	97.8
Kuwait	96.5
Iran	89.7
Venezuela	77.7
Russia	48.6
U.S.	30.4
Libya	29.5
Mexico	26.9

Top world oil exporters—Millions of barrels per day, Jan.–May 2002

Saudi Arabia	6.6
Russia	4.8
Norway	3.1
Iran	2.4
Venezuela	2.3
UAE	.9
Nigeria	1.8
Mexico	1.6
Iraq	1.6
Kuwait	1.6

Sources: U.S. Department of Energy, British Petroleum, International Energy Agency

Leo Drollas, chief economist at the Center for Global Energy Studies in Oxford, England, says the Saudis and other oil-producing giants will try to drive a hard bargain at a price that neither Bush nor Kerry is prepared to pay—a shift away from Washington's strong backing of Israel.

"The Saudis are interested in getting a solution to the Palestinian problem, saying to the United States that it must do something to press Israel to move toward peace," said Drollas. "The administration would prefer to live with high oil prices than to give in to the Saudis."

Amy Myers Jaffe, an oil analyst at the James Baker Institute for Public Policy at Rice University in Houston, points out another reason that oil prices are likely to stay high—the Saudi royal family needs to maximize revenue from the country's reserves (the world's largest) to help pay for a crumbling welfare state that has failed to satisfy a fast-growing population.

"In Saudi Arabia today, concern about public opinion is much higher than in the past, because the Saudis are facing a huge demographic challenge," she said. "In the 1970s, there were only 7 million people living in the country, but that number has tripled, and it looks likely to double in the next decade. People are generationally poorer than their parents, and the chances are that their children will be poorer still."

"The administration would prefer to live with high oil prices than to give in to the Saudis."—Leo Drollas, Center for Global Energy Studies

---

The rest of OPEC. Jaffe said other producers, like the Saudis, have no incentive to lower prices. "OPEC's basic position is that in the past few years, the international economy has been very resilient to upward movement in oil prices, and the U.S. economy is booming despite $35-per-barrel oil. The producers say, 'In the 1990s, no one did anything to help us, when oil was $10 per barrel.'"

The leader least likely to heed the entreaties of the administration is Venezuela's leftist president, Hugo Chavez, who has repeatedly accused Washington of trying to overthrow him. But Kerry also has little leverage because two weeks ago, he attacked Bush from the right, accusing the president of coddling Chavez and saying the United States should increase pressure on him.

Conservation is a hard sell. American drivers are buying ever-greater quantities of SUVs and light trucks, according to March sales figures. Cars and trucks averaged 20.4 miles a gallon in the 2002 model year, the lowest point since 1980.

Kerry has cautiously indicated support for improving fuel-efficiency standards on new cars and trucks, but that very caution illustrates just how difficult it is for American politicians to preach conservation.

Kerry's campaign Web site says he supports an increase in the corporate average fuel economy standards, known as CAFE, from the current average of 27.5 miles per gallon to 36 miles per gallon by 2015, for an estimated savings of 2 million barrels of oil daily—which, the site says, is "about the same amount we import from the Persian Gulf."

But two top Michigan Democrats, Gov. Jennifer Granholm and Sen. Carl Levin, have lobbied Kerry to scrap the proposal. They say he has agreed, but Kerry has kept a pointed silence about it on the campaign trail. Kerry aides insist that the 36 miles-per-gallon target remains his official policy.

Amending CAFE standards is controversial because of its effect on jobs and safety. U.S. automakers argue that raising standards would benefit foreign-based rivals, whose average vehicle sizes are smaller than those of American firms. Critics say the easiest way to improve fuel economy is to make lighter vehicles, but they have higher accident injury rates than heavier vehicles.

Many conservatives say they are ready to attack Kerry if he vocally advocates amending CAFE standards on the campaign trail.

"Increasing CAFE standards is not practical for today, tomorrow or the next 20 years," said Charli Coons, an energy analyst at the conservative Heritage Foundation in Washington. "If Kerry wants to get up on the stump and say that Americans' lives ought to be endangered by forcing them to drive smaller cars, I think he'll find out that voters strongly disagree."

In 2002, Kerry and Sen. John McCain, R-Ariz., proposed an almost identical package of fuel-economy improvements, but their amendment to that year's energy bill went down to a 62-to-38 defeat in the Senate.

Although scientists and environmentalists agree that improved fuel economy is the best way to reduce U.S. oil imports, they say Kerry's claim of "energy independence" is exaggerated.

Scientists at the American Council for an Energy-Efficient Economy, a widely respected Washington think tank that carried out data analysis for the Kerry and McCain legislation in 2002, estimate that a 36 miles-per-gallon target would save only about 1.3 million barrels per day, less than Kerry's claim of 2 million. Furthermore, current U.S. imports from the Persian Gulf of 2.5 million barrels per day are projected to increase to at least 3.3 million barrels per day by 2015—meaning that Kerry's proposal would cut only 37 percent of American imports from that region.

"Increased CAFE standards is environmentally worth doing, but it's a bit simplistic to say it would give us independence from the Saudis," said William Prindle, deputy director at the energy council. "In fact, their dominance would tend to increase, because reduction of demand would drive prices down, leaving the Saudis in a better position because they are the lowest-cost producer. That could put the Middle East more firmly in the driver's seat."

China. Neither candidate will be able to prevent China's unquenchable thirst for oil from boosting prices. Experts say that a major factor behind the rise in oil prices over the past year—at a time when prices were expected to collapse as postwar Iraq resumed exporting—is the astronomical rise in imports by China.

With 1.3 billion people, a booming economy, 70 percent annual growth in auto sales yet stagnant domestic oil production, China has become highly dependent on foreign oil. Chinese oil imports rose 31 percent last year, making the country the No. 2 petroleum user after the United States, and its imports are expected to soar by as much as 40 percent this year.

"Chinese demand has really buoyed oil prices, and will continue to do so for the foreseeable future," said Fareed Mohamedi, chief economist at PFC Energy Corp., an oil-industry consulting firm in Washington. "China has become a major player on the oil markets, and its strategic needs will form a big part of world geopolitics of this century."

> *Most analysts say that . . . American consumers will remain umbilically joined with the Persian Gulf— through the gas pump.*

Bush's concessions to the auto industry. In February, the administration extended for four years a policy that allows auto manufacturers to gain fuel-economy credits for so-called dual-fueled vehicles, which can run on ethanol. Experts call the program a boondoggle, saying such vehicles almost always run on ordinary gasoline. The measure is estimated to increase national oil consumption by about 158,000 barrels per day by 2008.

The administration also is proposing a change in CAFE standards, eliminating the requirement that fuel-economy levels be calculated for the average of an automaker's entire fleet and instead creating requirements by weight category. Analysts say this change would cause automakers to switch to heavier vehicles with lower fuel-economy standards—thus leading to a reduction of overall fuel economy.

Auto workers, who long have opposed CAFE standards, have joined with environmentalists to fight the proposal, arguing that it would cause automakers to shift production of smaller, less profitable cars to low-wage foreign nations.

"The Bush administration's proposal would destroy American jobs, reduce fuel economy and increase global warming emissions—and add to the burdens of an already struggling auto industry," wrote Sierra Club Executive Director Carl Pope and United Auto Workers President Ron Gettlefinger in a February opinion piece in the *New York Times*.

Most analysts say that while high gasoline prices are likely to produce rhetorical sparks on the campaign trail, American consumers will remain umbilically joined with the Persian Gulf—through the gas pump.

"There are important differences between the candidates on energy, but don't expect any reduction in our dependence on the Middle East any time soon," said Jaffe. "The Saudis' dominance of the oil markets is likely to increase for decades to come."

VI. Alternative Fuels

Editors' Introduction

Since the 1970s, American politicians have been urging us to find alternatives to imported oil, which has forced us to rely on foreign nations for fuel. Environmentally conscious individuals have also advocated that we reduce pollution-causing emissions. However, finding effective, cost-efficient solutions to the problem of expensive, unclean gasoline has proved difficult. Automobile manufacturers have tried electric cars, diesel vehicles, hydrogen fuel cells, and now hybrids. Some of their efforts have proved more successful than others, but, at the insistence of conscientious consumers, automakers are still trying.

Eric Minton provides "The Lowdown on Hybrids," detailing the most recent crop of hybrid cars—vehicles that combine internal combustion gas engines and electric motors to produce low emissions and high mileage per gallon. The motor and the engine are both connected to the wheels by the same transmission and work in tandem, their coordination controlled by computer. Three prominent heralds of the "age of environmentally conscious vehicles" are the Honda Civic and Insight and the Toyota Prius, which, thus far, have been quite popular, despite the fact that they cost approximately $3,000–$5,000 more than regular gasoline-powered cars.

John O'Dell also discusses hybrids in his article "Waving Yellow Flag on 'Green' Hybrid Vehicles," pointing out that, although hybrids are decidedly more eco-friendly than normal cars, their marketing is somewhat misleading. According to Prius, Civic, and Insight owners, the vehicles regularly average 10 to 20 miles per gallon less than advertised. Also, without federal tax breaks, it takes about 20 years to break even if a consumer buys a hybrid instead of a conventional car.

In "The Hydrogen Highway: Hype or a Happening?" Larry E. Hall examines the uncertain future of hydrogen fuel cell vehicles. Although there are currently more than 125 of this kind of auto in development, industry experts predict that it will be at the very least a decade before they will be available to the public. The subject of hydrogen made the headlines in 2003, when President George W. Bush asked for Congressional approval of $1.2 billion for the development of a hydrogen economy in his State of the Union address. However, there remain problems in the development of viable hydrogen cars, such as the difficulty of isolating a pure source of hydrogen and building a new distribution system to allow for convenient refueling of hydrogen vehicles.

Greg Schneider's article, "The Electric-Car Slide," focuses on a different source of power: electricity. Unlike hydrogen fuel cells, though, electric cars are not being developed for future use; rather, they are being removed from the market. The 1990s saw a push for the environmentally sound electric cars, but many felt that the cars were not economically feasible and inconvenient to recharge. However, some electric car owners are so attached to their electric cars that they are begging to extend their leases. Not only are electric car owners convinced of their vehicles' viability, but some scientists also have faith in the cars, insisting that "the auto industry is retreating just as progress in battery technology is finally pushing toward a breakthrough." Unfortunately for proponents of the vehicles, the future does not look promising for electric cars.

It seems that the future of the diesel engine is on shaky ground as well. While diesels made up 35 to 40 percent of Europe's 2002 fleet of new cars, their market share in the United States is only .26 percent. In "The Diesel," Dennis Simanaitis examines the pros and cons of diesel engines. Diesel engines cost an average of $1,300 to $2,000 more per engine than their gasoline-using counterparts, and diesel produces certain emissions of nitrogen oxides, particles of oil, and potentially cancer-causing soot. On the other hand, diesel is cheaper than gasoline in Europe, and gets approximately 30 percent better mileage. However, while many Europeans are staunch defenders of their diesel vehicles, with gas prices cheaper in the United States and debatable environmental benefits, others doubt that diesels will ever take the country by storm.

The Lowdown on Hybrids

By Eric Minton
GEICO Direct, Fall 2003

Jim Lents sounds like a character in a personal-testimony commercial for his hip new car. He's telling about how he went camping and fit all his stuff in the trunk. He kept pace with every car going up the curving mountain road—even passing some. "The performance was there—even better than my minivan and pickup truck," Lents relates.

Why should these facts be so highly touted? Because it's not performance or styling that makes Lents' new car hipper than the rest. His is a Honda Civic hybrid, one of several hybrid models in the U.S. market that combines a gas engine and electric motor to produce a high-miles-per-gallon, low-emission drive. The Civic, which came out in 2002, joins Honda's Insight and the Toyota Prius to herald a new age of environmentally conscious vehicles.

The Old and the New

Electric cars were supposed to be the transportation of the future, but they failed to catch hold in the present. Consumers were turned off by top speeds of 70 mph, by a steep price tag and, primarily, by the 80- to 100-mile range of the batteries, which would then need to be recharged. Intended only for short trips, most electric cars also lacked much hauling capability.

Hybrids use an electric motor and internal-combustion engine working in tandem, both connected to the wheels by the same transmission. The motor and engine coordination is computer-controlled. While each manufacturer has its own specific technology, generally speaking the electric motor helps power the car in idle and during acceleration. The gas engine takes over while cruising. It powers the drive-train and helps to recharge the electric motor's battery while doing so. When braking or decelerating, the electric motor provides braking torque, which also generates electricity, and energy normally wasted in the brake shoes is recovered. Some hybrids, such as Ford's Escape SUV, also can operate in the electric-only mode.

Reprinted with permission of GEICO and K.L. Publications from the Fall 2003 *GEICO Direct*. May not be reproduced without permission.

Incentive Programs

Does it pay to have an environmentally friendly vehicle?

In the case of hybrids, the tandem electric motor and gas engine add as much as $3,000 to a vehicle's sticker price. In the case of other alternative fuel vehicles, such as electric cars, the price can be higher.

However, to spur purchases of cleaner cars, a number of federal and state tax and rebate incentives have been legislated.

The U.S. government offers a one-time federal income tax deduction for the purchase of a new hybrid. Through the 2003 tax year the deduction is $2,000. It drops to $1,500 for 2004, $1,000 for 2005, and $500 for 2006.

Plans call for an eventual phase-out, but Congress is considering extending the incentive, as well as establishing a tax-credit program for advanced technology vehicles, a group that includes hybrids.

States also offer a variety of rebate programs and incentives—financial and otherwise—to encourage the purchase or lease of hybrids. For information on individual states:

- Visit the "Financial Incentives" section of the Vehicle Buyer's Guide for Consumers at *www.ccities.doe.gov/vbs/*.

- Call the Department of Energy's National Alternative Fuels Hotline at 1-800-423-1363.

- Check with your car dealer, local tax office or your Department of Motor Vehicles.

The distance range is typical of any high-mpg vehicle. And rather than plugging in to "refuel, " like traditional electric vehicles, drivers pump gas just as they would for any other car. The technology adds only about $3,000 to the car's sticker price, but part of this additional cost may be recouped through tax-incentive programs.

"The thing that makes hybrids remarkable is that their operation is seamless to the consumer," says Kevin Mills, director of the Clean Car Campaign at Environmental Defense. "You've got a computer that's optimizing how much you use the electric motor versus the internal

combustion engine. You don't do anything different, and the experience is more pleasant and more convenient because you can go half again-as-far on a tank of gas."

Sales Are on the Rise

Sales numbers point to the cars' potential popularity. For example, in 2000, when Toyota introduced the Prius to the U.S. market, the manufacturer allotted 12,000 units a year.

"We sold every one we got," says Sam Butto, senior product news administrator at Toyota. "We were having trouble getting one for display purposes for dealerships."

In 2002, Toyota raised the production allotment for the U.S. to 17,000 cars, and in 2003 to 20,000. To date, Toyota has sold more than 45,000 Priuses in the United States and set a monthly sales record for the car in March 2003, selling 2,532. These numbers pale when compared to 400,000 Camrys per year, but only one factory is producing the Prius, and the location literally cannot produce them fast enough. "We're selling all we can get," Butto notes.

Unlike many of the purely electric forebears, Toyota styled the Prius to look like any economy car on the market. Honda took the next step with the Civic by putting hybrid technology in an existing model line.

> *"We need cleaner cars, and hybrids fit that bill."*—Jim Lents, University of California, Riverside

The next step is slated for some larger vehicles by several manufacturers. In late summer of 2004, Ford is planning to introduce the Escape SUV hybrid; DaimlerChrysler has announced the production of a hybrid Dodge Ram pick-up truck; and Lexus is readying to sell a hybrid RX330 luxury SUV. General Motors has targeted the 2005 model year for introduction of the hybrid Saturn VUE utility vehicle.

Does the Technology Work?

Jim Lents, more than just about anyone else, is aware of his car's most important feature. He served for 11 years as executive officer of the South Air Quality Management District in California, and for the past six years he has been director of the Atmospheric Processes and Policy Laboratory at the University of California at Riverside. Among his lab's many air quality research projects is a test of hybrids and other low-emission cars to gauge their engines' efficiency.

"For the first 10,000 miles, they are holding up to their claims of low emissions," he says. "Next is to find out if they hold up between 10,000 and 50,000 miles." The research will require a few more years.

Lents specifically shopped for a hybrid when he decided to purchase a new car. "I like the concept so I was set on getting it," he explains. "We need cleaner cars, and hybrids fit that bill. I'm seriously concerned about world resources and global warming. Fuel economy means you're putting out a lot less carbon dioxide."

Where Hybrids Rule

Concern for the environment also spurred Gavin and Sally Wuttken to purchase a Toyota Prius. Both work at the Monterey Bay Aquarium in Monterey, Calif, and they are among more than two dozen aquarium staff members who have bought Priuses.

The Wuttkens are sold on more than the car's fuel-economy and low emissions. "The turning radius is tight; it's fast; you have tons of room; it's probably the same performance as any two-liter car, " Gavin says. Even maintenance differs little. Batteries are built to last the life of the vehicle and warrantied for eight years. Replacing them currently costs about $1,500, which compares favorably to any major drive-train replacement, according to the couple. That cost will likely diminish as technology and development methods improve, according to Toyota.

There are some differences, though. The Prius is heavier than typical cars of its class, so tire pressure becomes even more important.

Hybrid drivers also have to adjust to the gas engine shutting off when brakes are applied and the quiet electric motor takes over. "When it shuts off at an intersection, it's kind of a strange thing," Wuttken relates. Because the car uses the electric motor at low speeds, such as in parking lots, pedestrians don't hear it either, he adds. "They'll step right in front of you, so you have to drive more defensively," Wuttken says.

Safety and Mileage

As for safety, as of press time the National Highway Traffic Safety Administration (NHTSA) has crashtested the Honda Insight and Toyota Prius, as well as the original Civic sedan. It has the same chassis, body and safety features of the Civic hybrid, on which specific tests have not yet been performed.

Lents has his own personal story to tell about safety. His wife was rear-ended on the freeway when their hybrid Civic was just two weeks old. "The guy hit her pretty hard, smashed the whole trunk in," he relates. I thought they might total the car, but they fixed it and you can't tell the difference." His wife, meanwhile, didn't suffer even minor whiplash in the accident.

The hybrids come with digital dashboard illustrations of the engine controls so the driver can see which engine is engaged and how much energy is regenerating the battery. The Prius also has a dashboard display of the average miles per gallon.

The Wuttkens average about 45 mpg in their Prius, while Lents averages about 47 mpg in the Civic. According to manufacturers, mileage for the three models ranges from 48 to 57 mpg in the city and from 45 to 56 mpg on the highway. Unlike most cars, mileage averages for hybrids are generally inverted—meaning the vehicles get better mileage in city traffic because the electric motor provides the power for more of that type of driving. Consequently, hybrids are best-suited for people who do a lot of city driving.

Insuring a Hybrid

"There's no difference whatsoever to insure a hybrid," explains Jim Hit, GEICO's vice president of underwriting and product management. Vehicles with new technology and safety features go through the same industry analysis and evaluation by the Insurance Services Organization (ISO) as any other vehicle.

That's part of what determines costs to insure vehicle, Hitt explains. "If it becomes more expensive to replace a fuel cell, that will be taken into consideration," he says.

How Popular Will They Be?

Will hybrid popularity extend through suburbia to the American heartlands? Recently fluctuating gas prices may have some impact, but only the future will tell.

The National Transportation Research Center at Oak Ridge National Laboratory in Tennessee has conducted focus groups on the topics of fuel-economy and the environmental impact of automobiles.

"When people do consider the environment, it's pretty far down on the list," says Bo Saulsbury, a research associate. "When they think fuel economy, it's pretty much from an economic standpoint. They're still thinking of price; they're still thinking of styling. Another factor that rates high is vehicle function." Hybrids are the first alternative fueled cars to meet those standards.

"I expected to pay some performance penalty when I bought the vehicle but was pleased to find out I had to sacrifice none of that," says Lents.

Waving Yellow Flag on "Green" Hybrid Vehicles

By John O'Dell
Los Angeles Times, March 7, 2004

Arriving at the Kodak Theatre for the Academy Awards, actors Tim Robbins and Susan Sarandon clambered out of a Toyota Prius hybrid. Other stars aimed to make environmental statements by pulling up in gas-and-electric-powered Priuses, including Robin Williams and nominees Marcia Gay Harden and Keisha Castle-Hughes.

It was a public relations coup for Toyota Motor Corp. Japan's biggest automaker and rival Honda Motor Co. are the only companies that sell hybrid-powered vehicles in the United States. And sales are booming, as people flock to showrooms, figuring that hybrids will save them lots of money, especially with gasoline prices so high.

But consumer advocates say the marketing glosses over a few things, including the true operating cost of the cars, despite their fabled fuel economy. "If you're looking at this purely as a pocketbook decision, the hybrid won't work," says Gabriel Shenhar, senior auto test engineer for *Consumer Reports* magazine, although he has no quarrel with the hybrids' environmental credentials.

The three main reasons:

- Although the Prius and Honda's Civic and Insight hybrids do get terrific gas mileage, in real-world use they rarely match the extraordinary fuel economy the Environmental Protection Agency gets on its test circuit.

  The EPA rates the 2004 Prius at 60 miles per gallon in city driving and 51 mpg on the highway. The agency says Honda's 2004 Civic Hybrid gets 48 mpg city and 47 highway, and its two-seat Insight is rated at 61 mpg in the city and 68 on the open road.

  But *Consumer Reports'* testers measured only 44 miles per gallon in combined city and highway driving for the new Prius for an upcoming review, Shenhar notes. Several owners of the Civic Hybrid told *The Times* that their cars average in the low 40s per gallon in daily use, and one super-commuter who drives 200 miles a day in his Honda Insight says he averages 52 mpg.

- The federal government is gradually rolling back the tax deduction hybrid buyers can claim—it was $2,000 last year but $1,500

Copyright 2004, *Los Angeles Times*. Reprinted with permission.

this year. Unless Congress renews it, the deduction will keep declining until it disappears in 2007.

Without the tax break, hybrids cost significantly more than conventionally powered counterparts. The Toyota Prius' $20,510 sticker price is $4,400 more than that of a top-of-the-line, gasoline-fueled Toyota Corolla. The Honda Civic Hybrid, at $20,650, is $2,300 more than a top-end Honda Civic EX model.

So even with a hybrid's fuel savings, it can take years to erase the price difference. And if tax rebates are omitted, Shenhar figures, it will take about 20 years to break even if a consumer buys a Civic Hybrid instead of a conventional Civic EX.

- Analysts at Internet car shopping and information service Edmunds.com say the technology that makes hybrids appealing is improving so quickly that today's vehicles are likely to depreciate faster than conventional cars as new hybrids arrive.

"State-of-the-art today might not be so new when trade-in time comes three of four years from now," says Karl Brauer, editor in chief at Santa Monica-based Edmunds.

Edmunds's, "true-cost-to-own" formula shows that because of depreciation, a Prius or Civic Hybrid probably would cost $1,000 more over a five-year period than a comparable Corolla or conventional Civic.

What's more, the life span of the hybrids' expensive high-voltage battery packs is an issue that occasionally raises concerns. California and five other states require hybrids to be covered by a manufacturer's warranty for 10 years or 150,000 miles.

Spokesmen for Toyota and Honda say they have not yet had a claim for replacement of the massive battery packs—which are as wide as the cars themselves and carry a list price of about $3,000. The price is expected to decline as battery technology improves. Toyota engineers have talked about $1,000 replacement costs a few years from now.

"We expect the batteries to outlive the warranties," says Gunnar Lindstrom, head of marketing for alternative-fuel vehicles at American Honda Motor Co. in Torrance.

In rare cases when a hybrid isn't used for months at a time, the main high-voltage battery pack can drain. Hybrid enthusiast Declan Joyce says his 2001 Prius was involved in an accident late last year and then sat in the body shop for several months. When the repairs were finished, the shop had to wait two extra days for Toyota to deliver the only high-voltage Prius recharger in Southern California before his car could be started.

Market Is Growing

Still, with regular-grade gas at $2.20 a gallon and climbing, battery worries and ownership costs don't seem to weigh on shoppers' minds.

Toyota Motor Sales USA boosted its 2004 sales target for the Prius to 47,000 units, up from 30,000 last year. American Honda Motor expects to sell about 20,000 Civic Hybrids this year and about 1,000 Insights, which have been slow sellers because they are two-seaters with little room for cargo.

Both Torrance-based importers will add new hybrids to their line-ups in the next year. Their Japanese rival Nissan Motor Co. and No. 1 and 2 American automakers General Motors Corp. and Ford Motor Co. all have plans to introduce hybrids of their own in the next two years.

Sharon Wrathall, who covers 195 miles a day commuting from Bakersfield to her job at a Burbank public relations firm, says she averages 46 miles per gallon in her 2004 Prius. And Kim Tsuchida, 28, a software developer for Warner Bros. Entertainment in Burbank, says her 2004 Honda Civic Hybrid delivers about 42 miles per gallon on her commute from West Los Angeles.

> *It's hard to look at vehicle mileage and make an economic argument for going hybrid.*

Both say they wouldn't trade their hybrids for conventional models. Their harshest criticism: Their cars' stereo systems aren't very good.

At the same time, they say they are disappointed they can't get the same mileage the automakers like to advertise.

In fact, the EPA has received complaints from owners about the discrepancies and has discussed redesigning the mileage test for hybrids.

Money Isn't Everything

Duane Allen, owner of two first-generation Priuses, agrees that it's hard to look at vehicle mileage and make an economic argument for going hybrid.

The 57-year-old electronics engineer averages about 12,000 miles a year in his 2003 Prius. At today's gas prices, he would save about $250 over what he would spend if he drove his wife's new Toyota Scion xB, which gets about 34 mpg on the highway.

The Prius cost about $5,000 more than the Scion, though, "so there's no net savings at all," he points out.

But Allen, like most other hybrid users, said he enjoys the psychic rewards of having to gas up only half as often as his neighbors do. He also likes "knowing that I'm causing a lot less pollution as I drive down the freeway."

As "super-low-emission vehicles" with zero evaporative emissions from the gas tank and fuel lines, the Prius and Civic hybrids earn the best emissions rating that California issues—though 17 conventionally powered cars do too.

Hybrids do pump out less carbon dioxide than gasoline-only low-emission vehicles, because they shut down their gas engines at stoplights. And the Prius can even run in all-electric mode for several miles if conditions are right, so it's "greener" than a conventional car.

"That's what makes it worthwhile," says Prius driver Wrathall. "I'm doing something good for the environment, and I'm getting more than twice the mileage I got with my old car."

The Hydrogen Highway:
Hype or a Happening?

By Larry E. Hall
MSN Autos, October 16, 2003

Three questions everybody wants answered about hydrogen fuel cell vehicles today are: how soon, how good, and how much? The answers are: who knows, it's hard to say, and it's anybody's guess.

The fact of the matter is, fuel cell vehicles for general consumption are still years away from showing up in car dealer showrooms. Yes, there are upwards of 125 of these vehicles that are being tested on streets and highways around the globe, including buses, and a delivery van; however, a real world hydrogen fuel cell electric car for everyday driving is still a long way off.

Which brings up another question. Is this trip down the hydrogen highway just hype, or is it a happening?

Too Much Hype, Too Soon?

Ask any car company that has a development program for hydrogen fuel cell vehicles when consumers can expect to drive one, and there is a fairly pat answer—"around the end of this decade or a little longer."

Talk with oil companies, who are now referring to themselves as energy companies with plans to play a major role in the production and distribution of hydrogen, and their estimates of when hydrogen might be readily available to fuel cars and their responses are different, but also pretty much in concert—"over the next few decades" is their guesstimate.

Hmmm, that's a fairly large disparity between the two time projections. Whichever answer is closest to being correct, it confirms that the arrival of hydrogen fuel cell cars is still a long way off.

Yet, recently the media began to hail the attributes of fuel cell vehicles, romancing the public with sound bites and pseudo-facts about zero emissions, cleaning the air, and quiet, efficient, environmentally friendly transportation.

Automakers have been actively exploring hydrogen as an alternative fuel for more than 20 years, and began serious research into fuel cells starting in the early 1990s, with only occasional mentions by the press. The recent fanfare has been fueled by several events that occurred in short succession.

Article by Larry E. Hall from *MSN Autos* October 16, 2003. Copyright © *MSN Autos*. Reprinted with permission.

Courtesy of Michael A. Messina

The X-Trail fuel cell vehicle, manufactured by Nissan.

First, last September at the 2002 Paris Motor Show, General Motors unveiled the Hy-Wire, a fuel cell concept car that featured a "skateboard" chassis and electric drive-by-wire controls. The futuristic looking Hy-Wire became a live wire, with its image appearing on TV screens, computer screens, and in newspapers and magazines.

Three months later in December, Honda and Toyota made headlines when they announced that the first hydrogen fuel cell passenger vehicles in the United States were hitting the roads in California.

Honda handed the keys to five of its four-passenger FCX vehicle to the city of Los Angeles for long-term test research; Toyota delivered the first two of six FCHVs, a so-called fuel cell hybrid based on the Highlander SUV, to the University of California, Irvine, and the University of California, Davis, for the same purpose. Both companies said the deliveries were historic.

The Bush Push

Then in January, the subject became front page news. In his State of the Union address, President Bush asked for Congressional approval of $1.2 billion toward the development of a hydrogen economy. The money would be used for commercially viable hydrogen fuel cells to power vehicles, homes and businesses that produce no pollution and no greenhouse gases.

The President suggested that "the first car driven by a child born today [2003] could be powered by hydrogen, and pollution free."

Over the next few days, fueled by sound bites and headlines, hydrogen fuel cell vehicles became a topic of discussion around the office water cooler and at social gatherings.

Not everyone assesses the widespread coverage of fuel cell cars as hype. Alan Traub, the executive director of science laboratories at General Motors views the exposure as beneficial to the public. "When new technologies and new ideas, like fuel cells, like the Hy-Wire, emanate, there is a lot of media attention, but that exposure brings forth discourse that wouldn't happen otherwise."

George Peterson, president of Auto Pacific, an automotive marketing and consulting firm in Tustin, Calif., views the publicity on fuel cell vehicles as perhaps setting up consumers with high expectations for a technology that may never become reality, not unlike the attention given to electric vehicles in the 1990s.

Peterson does believe the information about fuel cells is better delivered, however, and that consumers are aware that vehicles are still a long way off.

Many opponents of hydrogen powered vehicles ... say it may not be good science or technology.

Critics and Cynics

For every hydrogen and fuel cell advocate, there's a critic or cynic. Many opponents of hydrogen powered vehicles, including those in the environmental community, say it may not be good science or technology.

For example, the ideal way to obtain hydrogen is to separate it from water by using alternative energy sources like wind and solar power because the hydrogen is pure. However, that is not yet cost effective.

So, the most likely source for some time would be "transition" hydrocarbon fuels such as natural gas, gasoline and methanol, whereby hydrogen is made by using a "reformer."

Researchers at the Massachusetts Institute of Technology say this method uses substantial energy and emits greenhouse gases.

Others cite the enormous cost of building a new distribution infrastructure to make refueling with hydrogen as convenient as today's corner gas station. Still others are concerned about safety—storage of hydrogen at the fill-up location and on-board the vehicle.

A confessed cynic is J. D. Power and Associates auto analyst, Walter McManus. "Change is gradual, and change will come only with real pressure," said McManus. "Right now, there is no pressure to switch from petroleum to fuel cells because gasoline is still cheap, and there doesn't seem to be a shortage of oil supplies."

Outspoken fuel cell critic Todd Turner, president of automotive consulting firm Car Concepts in Thousand Oaks, Calif., says all the hoopla over fuel cell vehicles is premature and the technology is still experimental.

We've Been Down This Road Before

Like Peterson, McManus sees the rush towards fuel cells as a possible parallel to the electric vehicle panacea of the '90s.

The panic to produce electrics started in 1990 when California adopted rules that required car companies to sell "zero emission vehicles" (ZEVs)—two percent beginning in 1998, five percent by 2001, and 10 percent by 2003—or pull out of the state. With California representing 12 percent of U.S. car sales, the rush was on.

In 1991, Congressional bills were introduced to spend $60 million to jump start electric car development, promising an "automobile revolution" that would reduce air pollution and oil consumption.

General Motors wowed the press in 1993 with the Impact prototype two-seat electric car, capable of a zero to 60 mph time of eight seconds. By the time 1998 rolled around, every major automaker that sold cars in the U.S. had an electric vehicle available to lease, mostly to government or business fleets. Eventually, California eased off, and then cancelled the ZEV mandate. Only around 2,000 electric vehicles found their way to streets and highways.

Wait, What About Hydrogen Fueled Internal Combustion Engines?

Virtually all the fanfare about hydrogen and automobiles of late fixate on fuel cells. One automobile company has championed the internal combustion engine for more than two decades.

"For nearly 25 years, BMW has been the lone wolf in developing a hydrogen fueled internal combustion engine vehicle," said BMW Group spokesperson, David Buchko. "We have researched other hydrogen technologies extensively, and have a commitment to the hydrogen combustion engine."

BMW's approach is a bi-fuel system, using both hydrogen and gasoline. The company envisions a hydrogen powered BMW on the road by the end of this decade.

Recently, Ford unveiled a supercharged hydrogen combustion engine powered vehicle. The company says it is dedicated to the idea of fuel cell powertrains in mass produced consumer vehicles.

However, since fuel cells are not ready for production in the near term, Ford regards the hydrogen combustion engine as a "bridging" strategy to stimulate a hydrogen infrastructure and related technologies.

The Race Is On

Currently, nine automakers from around the world are showing off either a hydrogen fuel cell or hydrogen combustion engine passenger vehicle in the United States.

Four companies—BMW, General Motors, Honda and Toyota—are currently, or have just completed "real world" test research.

DaimlerChrysler and Ford have just announced similar programs that will begin in the next few months, while Hyundai, Nissan, and Volkswagen have yet to announce any plans.

Some industry analysts are giving GM the nod in the race to be the first to deliver affordable fuel cell vehicles to the public, and not just because they have a huge development budget.

The type of fuel cell that produces energy for vehicles, the proton exchange membrane (PEM), is also applicable for use in stationary power units that can produce electricity for home and commercial applications. GM plans to enter that market where the benefit is volume production of fuel cell components, which will help lower the cost of fuel cells for vehicles, giving GM a competitive cost advantage.

The fact that Honda and Toyota were first to deliver government certified fuel cell vehicles for commercial testing in the U.S. can't be overlooked.

Ben Knight, vice resident of Honda R&D in Torrance, Calif., believes the automaker's technology experience with hybrid, compressed natural gas and electric vehicles provides a competitive edge with fuel cell vehicles.

Of course, the other car companies also have similar technical knowledge of these vehicle systems and are transferring them to fuel cell vehicles.

Who would guess what, if any, head start DaimlerChrysler might gain with the delivery of 30 fuel cell buses this year in Europe?

The race down the hydrogen highway has started, but it's not an absolute sure bet that any of the contestants will ever finish.

Perhaps the retired chief executive of Ford Motor Co., Alex Troutman, said it best in a 1994 Forbes article about electric vehicles: "We've spent hundreds of millions on things that didn't work. When we spent the money, we didn't know they wouldn't work."

The Electric-Car Slide

By Greg Schneider
The Washington Post, October 22, 2003

Steven Dibner drove the thinking man's hot rod. Instead of roaring with power and guzzling gas, his car whispered along on rechargeable batteries.

But make no mistake, Dibner's all-electric GM coupe could zoom away from a stoplight with drag-strip speed. He was saving money on fuel, causing no pollution and "driving the coolest, sexiest, most interesting car on the road," said Dibner, a bassoonist with the San Francisco Symphony.

General Motors Corp. built 1,100 of the two-seater EV1s beginning in 1997, pushing electric-car technology further than it had ever gone in a mass-produced vehicle. But to the dismay of Dibner and other alternative-fuel advocates, GM has canceled the program and is confiscating all the cars.

The auto industry's electric-car movement—which gained momentum in the 1990s thanks to a push by California regulators—is now all but dead. GM and other major automakers are abandoning their efforts to produce a battery-powered car for the mass market.

Instead, they are focusing on hybrid vehicles that boost the mileage of a gasoline engine with the use of some electric power. Ultimately, the industry hopes—perhaps decades from now—to offer vehicles powered by hydrogen fuel cells, a fledgling auto technology that delivers power by converting hydrogen to water.

The death knell for pure electric cars sounded this summer when California's regulators, responding to industry arguments that battery power wasn't economically feasible, backed away from stringent antipollution rules that had accelerated the vehicles' development. Toyota Motor Corp., Honda Motor Co., Nissan Motor Co., Ford Motor Co. and DaimlerChrysler AG all have canceled electric-car programs this year.

GM is now taking back EV1s as their leases run out. Battery-power enthusiasts staged a mock funeral for their cars in July in a Hollywood cemetery, complete with a hearse and bagpipes.

Dozens of EV1 drivers have sent GM $500 checks to beg for more time, but the company returned their money. About 100 of the cars will go to the state of New York for research on battery performance in cold weather. A few others are going to museums, and the rest of the EV1 fleet will be scavenged for parts or scrapped.

© 2003, *The Washington Post*, reprinted with permission.

Automakers say that electric vehicles cost too much to manufacture and that batteries will never provide as much driving range as a full tank of gas. The internal-combustion engine simply has a lock on American driving habits—it is the rare car buyer, the reasoning goes, who will accept having to tether a vehicle to a power outlet for hours to refuel it when a quick visit to a gas pump is still possible.

But scientists who have spent careers working on batteries say the auto industry is retreating just as progress in battery technology is finally pushing toward a breakthrough. Battery life is extending rapidly, and electric cars' performance and styling have edged ever closer to their gas cousins. The mass market "could have battery-powered cars in five years or less," said Tom Gage, president of AC Propulsion Inc., a California company developing technology for electric cars.

What's needed, Gage said, is a commitment from just one major corporation to use its might to shove past the last few hurdles, such as manufacturing new batteries in big enough numbers to bring down their cost.

Battery supporters . . . insist that the promise of electric will yet bear fruit.

Battery supporters, whose ranks include major names from industry and science, insist that the promise of electric will yet bear fruit—in future hybrid vehicles that rely more on electricity than gasoline, in commercial uses such as fleets of delivery vans, and ultimately in a return to mass-market battery-powered cars.

"Some of us still believe in electric drive and pure battery power," said Robert C. Stempel, the former GM chairman and chief executive who helped start the EV1 program. Forced out in the early 1990s, Stempel now runs a company that develops batteries and alternative automotive technology.

"What goes around comes around," he said. "We'll see where they wind up eventually."

Electric cars are nothing new. In the late 1800s, electricity vied with steam and internal combustion for the top spot in new automotive technology. Henry Ford's wife drove electric cars, and the clean, quiet vehicles were cast as products for genteel society women.

But there was a problem that even Thomas Edison couldn't solve, and it has continually held back electric-car development: Batteries haven't been able to compete with the driving range of a full tank of gas.

In the late 1980s, GM seemed to find a way around the problem when it teamed with a California company called AeroVironment Inc. to build a solar-powered electric car for a race in Australia. Founded by legendary inventor Paul MacCready, the man whose Gossamer Albatross and Gossamer Condor aircraft set records for human-powered flight, AeroVironment helped design a vehicle so aerodynamic and energy-efficient that it blew away the competition and made world headlines.

The partnership eventually led to the design for the EV1, which current GM research-and-development chief Larry Burns said "remains the world's most efficient production vehicle."

The EV1's rear wheels were set closer together than the front, creating a teardrop shape with little wind resistance. Combined with new lightweight materials and electronic controls, the design overcame battery limitations to result in a vehicle that could go roughly 100 miles on a two-to-four-hour charge.

It also had no gears to shift and delivered full power instantly, so the EV1 accelerated from zero to 60 mph in 8.5 seconds—comparable to some Mustangs and performance cars. Test versions reached nearly 200 mph.

While the EV1 was being developed, the state of California was drawing up the nation's most stringent clean-air requirements—

"There is that whole collection of business interests that certainly don't want to see the gasoline-powered car disappear."—
Charles Hyde, historian, Wayne State University

---

requiring that 10 percent of new cars be emission-free by 2003. That pushed all automakers to develop electric vehicles, and quickly.

The backlash from the industry was ferocious. Car companies—and the oil industry—fought California's electric-car mandate "every way you can think of," said Jerry Martin, spokesman for the California Air Resources Board.

The firms lobbied state and federal lawmakers. They ran ads in newspapers and on television, warning consumers that the electric car mandate would drive up prices on all vehicles. Executives testified before the state board that battery technology wouldn't work. GM filed suit in 2001 to stop the state's plans and then embarked on a campaign of media interviews and statehouse lobbying to claim that electric cars wouldn't meet safety standards, wouldn't really contribute to clean air and had no viable consumer market.

"There is that whole collection of business interests that certainly don't want to see the gasoline-powered car disappear," said historian Charles Hyde, a professor at Wayne State University in Detroit. "I have a gut feeling that if electric cars really became more and more viable, you'd suddenly start to see gasoline prices really go down, to keep people in tow."

The political winds also turned against battery power. The Bush administration, where White House chief of staff Andrew H. Card Jr. is a former GM lobbyist, last year joined GM and Chrysler in a lawsuit against California's mandate. Also last year, the Department of Energy absorbed a battery research project into a bigger program to develop hydrogen fuel cells.

The new frontier is lithium-ion batteries—the kind that power cell phones and laptops.

Even as they fought California, though, carmakers had to begin offering electric vehicles to meet the state's emissions standards. The programs were small—Toyota leased or sold fewer than 300 RAV4 EVs, and Nissan leased just over 200 Altra EVs—but drivers who sought them out often became big fans.

"My wife and I both loved that car. It was the best car we ever had, for sure," said former EV1 driver Tom Dowling, 66, a retired bank worker from Folsom, near Sacramento.

Dibner, the San Francisco bassoonist, said he waited four years to get his EV1, which GM only leased out, not wanting to sell something it considered experimental.

"It was there, it was basically there," he said of the EV1's technology. "The quick acceleration was a miracle, a marvel."

But GM executives viewed the cars as a liability. One industry official said each EV1 cost the company about $80,000, including research and development costs; leasing them out at $350 a month was a money-losing proposition.

Building the EV1 was "so prohibitively expensive that to continue to market them at that level was financially untenable," said Chris Preuss, GM spokesman.

Gradually, California gave in to the industry's arguments. In April, the state's air quality board said it would accept large numbers of low-emission cars in place of a few with zero emissions. When GM and Chrysler dropped their lawsuit against the state's emissions policy in August, battery advocates saw the end of an era.

Burns, the GM research chief, said the company simply can't wait around for battery technology to improve. While there may be thousands of people who would be happy to overlook an EV1's limitations, he said, "you've got to get on a pathway where you can be thinking millions and tens of millions of vehicles."

Battery-powered cars may never reach that level of appeal because "gasoline is so very inexpensive," he said.

But MacCready, the AeroVironment scientist, said advances in a promising new area of battery technology could change that equation. Most electric cars have used ancient lead-acid batteries, and some progressed to nickel-metal hydride. The new frontier is lithium-ion batteries—the kind that power cell phones and laptops.

"Lithium [-ion batteries] will eventually be found to be the good substitute for gasoline-powered cars," MacCready said. Thanks to mass production in Asia, "the price is going down and the capability is going up, and researchers think that in another year they'll be up 50 percent from what they produce now in terms of energy and maybe double in two years," he said.

Lighter and more durable than their predecessors, lithium ion batteries have not yet been scaled up to car-battery size, but AC Propulsion has found a way around that. The San Dimas–based company, whose founder, Alan Cocconi, developed electric drive technology for the EV1, has built a car called the Tzero that's packed with 6,800 tiny cell phone batteries.

Designed for sports-car performance, the Tzero has a range greater than 300 miles, can go from zero to 60 mph in a neck-snapping 3.6 seconds—and costs $220,000. It's not a mass-market vehicle, but its designers believe it's a start.

"Originally, we had thought that with the car companies involved we could develop technology they'd be interested in buying. Now that they've essentially abandoned the market, we're looking at the possibility of marketing electric vehicles in low volume," said Gage, the AC Propulsion president.

At the same time, the Northern Virginia-based New Generation Motors Corp. is poised to announce a contract to mass-produce electric vehicles in India. While those cars will have a range and speed suitable for the average Indian's 15-mile commute, the technology could scale up to an EV1-like level, said Eric Takamura, director of manufacturing and engineering at New Generation.

"I think the battery technology is already there, as far as being practical for a typical commuter car," Takamura said. "It is really more of a costing issue. Without people actually going out there and buying it, you can't get the volumes up enough to bring down the cost."

The Diesel

BY DENNIS SIMANAITIS
ROAD & TRACK, MAY 2003

Diesels made up 35 percent of Europe's 2002 new-car fleet; they're expected to surpass 50 percent by 2010. Yet the diesel's market share in the U.S. is a minuscule 0.26 percent. What do Europeans know that we don't?

Or what do we know that they don't?

As a concept, Rudolf Diesel's compression ignition has been around since 1893. This was 15 years after Nikolaus Otto demonstrated the efficacy of a spark-ignited 4-stroke powerplant (and 54 years after Sir William Grove came up with the idea of a fuel cell). And, in fact, after years of relative neglect, diesel research and development activities have become front-burner at automakers and suppliers around the world. As a result, today's high-performance diesel is a far cry from those black-smoke belching clatterers of yore.

But are we Americans ready for them? And are today's diesels up to the realities of tomorrow's environmental issues, both here and elsewhere around the world?

Let's delve into fundamentals. Then we'll examine why so many Europeans favor diesels, why few in the U.S. share this enthusiasm, and how things are likely to change for both over the next five years.

Compression? Or Spark?

Fundamentals separating the two types of automotive engines are their means of ignition and their control of power. As its name implies, a spark-ignition engine uses a sparkplug to initiate combustion of its compressed gasoline/air mixture. By contrast, with a diesel, intake air is compressed, fuel is sprayed in, and ignition occurs through the heat of compression alone; thus, the term compression ignition, CI, versus spark ignition, SI.

Output of a spark-ignition engine is controlled by throttling the intake air while precisely balancing the amount of fuel. In a sense, an SI engine gets strangled at light load; it breathes most freely at wide-open-throttle (a relatively rare condition, even with us enthusiasts).

Article by Dennis Simanaitis from *Road & Track* May 2003. Copyright © Hachette Filipacchi Media U.S., Inc. Reprinted with permission.

By contrast, output of a CI engine is determined solely by the amount of fuel entering the combustion chamber; the air enters utterly unthrottled. Thus, a diesel has no added pumping losses at light load, and this is a fundamental reason for its frugality with fuel.

An SI engine's fuel/air mixture is compressed to around 1/10 of its intake volume; i.e., a compression ratio around 10:1. A typical CI engine's compression ratio is 20:1 or beyond. This higher compression enhances CI thermal efficiency; it also requires heavier components capable of withstanding greater combustion pressures.

It's estimated that a diesel offers a fuel-economy benefit of perhaps 25–30 percent.

With SI, the balancing act of air and fuel is important, because its combustion occurs ideally at a single particular air/fuel ratio, the stoichiometric one of 14:1 by weight. It can be finessed to run leaner; i.e., in lean-burn regimes of perhaps 30:1, but not without the complexities of direct injection and other tradeoffs. By contrast, in controlling output from full power to idle, a CI air/fuel mixture continues to ignite at 100:1 and leaner, another reason for a diesel's light-load efficiency.

In general, it's estimated that a diesel offers a fuel-economy benefit of perhaps 25–30 percent compared with an SI engine of similar displacement.

High End? Or Middle of the Barrel?

Both gasoline and diesel fuel are primarily petroleum products. There are biofuels of each type, but none has proven feasible in the large scale. Diesel fuel, like kerosene and jet fuel, is a middle distillate; gasoline, a lighter, high-end product.

Distressingly enough, in the old days when lamp and lubricating oils were the petroleum products in demand, high-end distillates were dumped into rivers and streams! Today, refineries are optimized for output, but still not without tradeoffs. The Europeans, for instance, refine so much diesel fuel that they end up with a glut of high-end product, some of this gasoline actually being sent our way. U.S. refineries favor cracking techniques that get more high-end out of the entire barrel. Ironically, one byproduct of this is an overproduction of diesel—but it's the wrong kind of diesel, with indifferent cetane and too much sulfur.

Just as octane measures the goodness of gasoline (actually, its knock resistance), cetane is the diesel's measure of quality. Briefly, cetane is inversely related to ignition lag; the higher the cetane, the less lag, the better the fuel. European diesel fuel is around 55 cetane; ours, more like 42–44.

Sulfur is the real problem, though, now and with future emissions controls, here and in Europe. Petroleum crudes vary from source to source. Benchmark Arab Light, for example, is a sweet crude (i.e., low in sulfur). Mayan and other Central American sources are considerably more sour. Refineries can finesse costs of crude supplies and sulfur removal, but only so far.

Sulfur in U.S. diesel fuel averages around 350 parts per million, 500 ppm being not unknown. In Europe, the absolute cap is 300 ppm; average levels are perhaps 175. In fact, Europeans already have low-sulfur diesel available with a maximum of 50 ppm, phasing down to 10 by 2005. We have low-sulfur diesel as well, but only in California. We also have similar national goals seen as crucial in meeting increasingly stringent (and immensely complex!) emissions-control standards phasing in between now and 2007. For example, by June 2006, 80 percent of U.S. diesel fuel sold by major refineries has a 15-ppm limit; this, rising to 100 percent by 2010.

HC, CO and CO_2? Or NO_x and Soot?

SI and CI powerplants differ radically in their engine-out (i.e., inherent) emissions. In particular, a diesel's hydrocarbon and carbon moNOxide emissions are much lower. And, as CO_2 output is essentially proportional to fuel consumption, a diesel exhibits a marked advantage in this regard as well. However, its exhaust still requires aftertreatment. And exhaust-stream differences complicate its downstream controls.

Diesel combustion is hotter than an SI's; thus it produces more oxides of nitrogen, NO_x. Yet its exhaust temperatures are considerably cooler, especially so if the engine is turbocharged (and thus extracting heat to drive the turbo). In fact, depending on load, diesel exhaust temperatures can be cooler by some 150 to 300 degrees Fahrenheit. Plus, as a diesel always operates with an excess of air (recall its unthrottled nature), there's always an overabundance of oxygen in its exhaust.

Lack of heat is bad news for just about any form of catalytic conversion. And a glut of oxygen is entirely the wrong condition for reducing NO_x. Ironically, even though a diesel's emissions characteristics are not unfavorable, its exhaust stream is not particularly amenable to downstream treatment.

And there's soot. Particulates, to give them their proper name, are an inherent byproduct of diesel combustion. And, note, I'm not talking about the black smoke of an ill-maintained diesel. Particulates are micro-sized, all the more injurious to our lungs and all the more difficult to trap. What's more, diesels generate an elemental quandary of particulates and NO_x: The hotter the combustion, the less particulates—but the more NO_x. There's excellent argument that diesel particulates—and not CO_2—constitute the most hazardous byproduct of automotive transportation.

Why Europeans Like Their Diesels

Part of the European love affair with the diesel makes a lot of sense. Part is what I perceive as Eurocentric posturing on environmental issues.

Largely because of taxation, motor fuels have always been exceptionally expensive over there. Thus, a diesel's inherently better fuel economy is a real attraction. Also,

> *The modern diesel engine has evolved into quite the engineering marvel.*

in many European countries, there are tax-invoked differences between diesel and gasoline prices. Belgium is the most striking case, with diesel going for the equivalent of $2.98/gal. versus gasoline priced at $4.02/gal. Curiously, though U.K. taxation is absolutely throttling, the situation there is similar to ours: gasoline is $4.71/gal.; diesel, $4.80/gal.

A Brit might consider a diesel for its fuel economy. A Belgian motorist would be most profligate not to buy a diesel.

Also, there's the larger issue of environmentalism—particularly CO_2 and its effect on global warming. I'll rant another time and place (this, after all, is what my Tech Tidbits column is for), but suffice to say the European Community has really bought into automotive CO_2 as a significant contributor to global warming. Governments offer incentives beyond fuel taxation for buying diesels. Also, in many countries, registration costs are keyed to engine size, and small-displacement turbodiesels provide what customers want—namely, torque.

Common Rails, Unit Injectors and Multiple Squirts

The modern diesel engine has evolved into quite the engineering marvel. Diesel technology was slow to adopt electronic engine management, but today's designs have evolved quickly and continue to exhibit a great deal of potential.

A common-rail diesel injection, for instance, operates at extremely high pressure, as high as 24,000 psi. This common rail is an accumulator as well as distributor, thus decoupling fuel pressure from engine rpm. Volkswagen opts for the same high-pressure decoupling, but with a different strategy. Its unit injectors combine pumping and injection in single assemblies, one per cylinder. With either approach, fuel injection can occur when and how engineers deem optimal.

As an example of its benefit, common-rail injection all but eliminates diesel clatter. With traditional CI, this ringing of the cylinder block is a response to irregular combustion in unexpected regions of the chamber (the diesel's equivalent of knock). Today's systems pre-condition the combustion through multiple-injection strategies, with one or two pilot injections at precise time and location. These pilot events are of extremely short duration, 40 microseconds, and involve tiny amounts of fuel, on the order of 1 mm^3.

Nor is the main injection a simple squirt. Piezoelectric injectors vary their nozzle geometry for super-fine, high-speed metering (see Tech Tidbits, August 2002). Arcane modeling techniques like genetic algorithms have suggested multiple events in this phase as well (see *Tech Tidbits*, February 2001).

What's more, post injections are used, one to complete the burn for reduced engine-out emissions, a second used intermittently to spike downstream HC, increasing temperatures for enhanced aftertreatment.

In the old days (10 years ago!), for each liter of displacement, diesels produced perhaps 45 bhp and around 70-80 lb.-ft. of torque. Today, figures are 75 bhp/liter and 110–120 lb.-ft./liter. It's no wonder that Europeans enjoy their diesels—so far.

Why Don't We Like Diesels?

The American experience with diesels has been, at best, a mixed one. Mercedes-Benz, Volkswagen and others have been in and out of

---

The American experience with diesels has been, at best, a mixed one.

---

the diesel market over the years. Oldsmobile soured the well in 1978 by coming to market with what turned out to be, in retrospect, a poorly-dieselized version of GM's 350-cu.-in. V-8. There never has been a price differential in favor of diesel fuel in this country. Last, heavy trucks—and truck stops—hardly added to diesel's passenger-car appeal.

Our emissions regulations haven't favored them (unlike in Europe, where standards are diesel- and gasoline-specific). As an example, California's South Coast Air Quality Management District has banned diesels from public vehicle fleets, and as recently as October 2002 a U.S. Circuit Court upheld this ban.

But Things Are Changing

Ironically enough, this court action was about the same time that the chairman of the California Air Resources Board spoke favorably of diesels in achieving the state's air quality objectives. And there has always been a dedicated band of knowledgeable diesel enthusiasts.

At the moment, Volkswagen's Golf, Jetta and New Beetle 1.9 TDIs are the only diesel-powered cars available here. In 2002, these turbocharged direct-injected VW diesels hardly dominated with only 15 percent of Golf, Jetta and New Beetle sales. However, whenever gasoline prices soar (as they inherently do from time to time), VW wishes it had scads more to sell. With this in mind, its Passat is getting a diesel later this year and the Touareg SUV will have a 5.0-liter V-10 TDI diesel in summer 2004.

Mercedes will bring us its E320 CDI (as in common-rail diesel injection) in 2004. Also in 2004, Jeep will offer its diesel Liberty already available outside North America. (By the way, there are also diesel PT Cruisers, built in Mexico but for Europe only. California-spec diesel fuel has to be trucked to the plant to fuel them; Mexican diesel would poison them with sulfur.)

Ford is studying plans for offering a diesel Focus within the next five years. Other U.S.-available diesels are concentrated toward the large end of the light-truck segment. Fully two out of three Ford F-Series Super Duty trucks, for instance, are diesel.

Diesel Clouds Ahead?

A lot of U.S. diesel activity is based on proposed hikes in the light-truck Corporate Average Fuel Economy standard phased in over 2005–2007. The class (which includes many pickups, mini-

---

Increasingly stringent emissions-control regulations challenge the diesel even more than its spark-ignition counterpart.

---

vans and SUVs) will likely face a 7.2-percent increase in mpg. Automakers are scrambling for SUV fuel efficiency, and dieselization is a straightforward 25–30 percent improvement.

There's a downside, though, both here and in Europe. Increasingly stringent emissions-control regulations challenge the diesel even more than its spark-ignition counterpart. In a sense, it's like the SI engine back in the 1970s, at the beginning of 3-way catalysis. Even with ultra-low-sulfur fuel, it's not clear that our coming NO_x and particulate regulations can be met.

And some pretty bizarre technology has been proposed. In response to Europe's Stage IV regulations, for instance, the PSA Peugeot Citroën HDI series has a silicon-carbide particulate filter that traps soot for some 250 miles, then requires a minute dose of rare-earth-derived compound to regenerate the device through superheating (around 850 degrees Fahrenheit!). A separate 1.3-gal. tank of this cerium-based Eolys additive needs replenishment every 50,000 miles or so.

Others are studying NO_x reduction in a catalytic converter fed a combination of diesel exhaust and urea, an ammonia-based compound.

CSI's Catalyzed Trap

Oxnard, California-based Catalytic Solutions Inc. has teamed up with Japan's Asahi Glass Co., Ltd. to develop a catalyzed particulate filter for meeting Europe's Stage IV and Stage V regulations. Asahi's silicon-nitride honeycomb has very small particle size, all the better for high surface area and optimal catalyst coating. The CSI catalyst coating uses relatively low levels of precious metals; this, to improve light-off temperature yet reduce cost.

Its duty cycle depends on soot accumulation within the honeycomb's tiny passages. Periodically, a backpressure sensor recognizes the need for eliminating the accumulated soot. Subtle changes in fuel injection enhance catalytic activity and cause a temperature rise in the catalyst, thus promoting this downstream soot combustion. CSI's catalyst enables rapid soot combustion during this regeneration event. Most important, this action is imperceptible to the driver.

I've written about CSI before (see "Technology Update: Clean the Sky! Wash the Wind!" April 2001; and *Tech Tidbits*, June 2001). This current research and development may once more "clean the sky and wash the wind," only this time, to the benefit of Rudolf Diesel's compression-ignition concept.

"Just as octane measures the goodness of gasoline . . . , cetane is the diesel's measure of quality." "The modern diesel engine has evolved into quite the engineering marvel." "There are also diesel PT Cruisers, built in Mexico but for Europe only."

Bibliography

Books

ACEEE's Green Book. Washington, D.C.: American Council for an Energy-Efficient Economy, 2002.

Berardelli, Phil. *The Driving Challenge: Dare to Be Safer and Happier on the Road*. Vienna, Va.: Nautilus Communications, 2001.

———. *Safe Young Drivers: A Guide for Parents and Teens*. 2nd ed. Vienna, Va.: Nautilus Communications, 2000.

Bradsher, Keith. *High and Mighty: SUVs—The World's Most Dangerous Vehicles and How They Got That Way*. New York: Public Affairs, 2003.

Burrington, Stephen H., and Veronika Thiebach. *Take Back Your Streets: How to Protect Communities from Asphalt and Traffic*. Boston: Conservation Law Foundation, 1998.

Committee for a Study of Transportation and a Sustainable Environment. *Toward a Sustainable Future: Addressing the Long-Term Effects of Motor Vehicle Transportation on Climate and Ecology*. Washington, D.C.: Transportation Research Board, National Research Council; National Academy Press, 1997.

DeWitt, John. *Cool Cars, High Art: The Rise of Kustom Kulture*. Jackson: University Press of Mississippi, 2001.

Edgerton, Jerry. *Car Shopping Made Easy: Buying or Leasing, New or Used: How to Get the Car You Want at the Price You Want to Pay*. New York: Warner Books, 2001.

Forman, Richard T. T., et al. *Road Ecology: Science and Solutions*. Washington, D.C.: Island Press, 2003.

Genat, Robert. *The American Car Dealership*. Osceola, Wis.: MBI, 1999.

Humphrey, Yveline Lecler, and Mario Sergio Salerno, eds. *Global Strategies and Local Realities: The Auto Industry in Emerging Markets*. New York: St. Martin's Press, 2000.

James, Leon. *Road Rage and Aggressive Driving: Steering Clear of Highway Warfare*. Amherst, N.Y.: Prometheus Books, 2000.

Kay, Jane Holtz. *Asphalt Nation: How the Automobile Took Over America, and How We Can Take It Back*. New York: Crown, 1997.

Koppel, Tom. *Powering the Future: The Ballard Fuel Cell and the Race to Change the World*. New York: Wiley, 1999.

Lascher, Edward L. *The Politics of Automobile Insurance Reform: Ideas, Institutions, and Public Policy in North America*. Washington, D.C.: Georgetown University Press, 1999.

Maynard, Micheline. *The End of Detroit: How the Big Three Lost Their Grip on the American Car Market*. New York: Currency/Doubleday, 2003.

McConnell, Curt. *Great Cars of the Great Plains*. Lincoln: University of Nebraska Press, 1995.

Motavalli, Jim. *Forward Drive: The Race to Build "Clean" Cars for the Future.* San Francisco: Sierra Club Books, 2000.

Peden, M., et al. *World Report on Road Traffic Injury Prevention.* Geneva, Switzerland: World Health Organization, 2004.

Penenberg, Adam L. *Tragic Indifference: One Man's Battle with the Auto Industry over the Dangers of SUVs.* New York: HarperBusiness, 2003.

Philips, Jerry J. *Who Pays for Car Accidents?: The Fault Versus No-fault Insurance Debate.* Washington, D.C.: Georgetown University Press, 2002.

Porter, Richard C. *Economics at the Wheel: The Costs of Cars and Drivers.* San Diego: Academic Press, 1999.

Rich, Curt. *Drive to Survive.* Osceola, Wis.: MBI, 1998.

Rifkin, Jeremy. *The Hydrogen Economy: The Creation of the Worldwide Energy Web and the Redistribution of Power on Earth.* New York: J. P. Tarcher / Putnam, 2002.

Riley, Robert Q. *Alternative Cars in the 21st Century: A New Personal Transportation Paradigm.* 2nd ed. Warrendale, Pa.: SAE International, 2004.

Romm, Joseph J. *The Hype About Hydrogen: Fact and Fiction in the Race to Save the Climate.* Washington, D.C.: Island Press, 2004.

Sandler, Martin W. *Driving Around the USA: Automobiles in American Life.* New York: Oxford University Press, 2003.

Saperstein, Robert, and Dana Saperstein. *Surviving an Auto Accident: A Guide to Your Physical, Emotional, and Economic Recovery.* Ventura, Calif.: Pathfinder Publishing of California, 1994.

Sutter, Paul. *Driven Wild: How the Fight Against Automobiles Launched the Modern Wilderness Movement.* Seattle: University of Washington Press, 2002.

Vaitheeswaran, Vijay V. *Power to the People: How the Coming Energy Revolution Will Transform an Industry, Change Our Lives, and Maybe Even Save the Planet.* New York: Farrar, Straus and Giroux, 2003.

Web Sites

This section offers the reader a list of Web sites that can provide additional information on car buying, automobile safety, and other information related to the auto industry. These Web sites also include links to other sites that may be of help or interest. Due to the nature of the Internet, the continued existence of a site is never guaranteed, but at the time of this book's publication, all of these Internet addresses were in operation.

Car Shopping Sites

The sites listed below enable car shoppers to research and buy new and used vehicles online. All or most of them also provide information on financing, warranties, anti-theft products, vehicle history reports, and obtaining car insurance. Some, such as CarsDirect and MSN Autos, also offer auto repair directories by which users may find service centers in their neighborhoods. For those wishing to sell their cars, eBaymotors can facilitate the process, while Autobytel.com offers the ability to post ads.

Autobytel.com *www.autobytel.com*

AutoTrader.com *www.autotrader.com*

CarMax *www.carmax.com*

CarsDirect *www.carsdirect.com*

eBaymotors *www.ebaymotors.com*

IntelliChoice *www.intellichoice.com*

MSN Autos *autos.msn.com*

Car Pricing Sites

The sites below provide information about the values of new and used cars, reviews and ratings, and advice about different models, financing, and auto insurance.

Edmunds *www.edmunds.com*

Kelley Blue Book *www.kbb.com*

Other Useful Sites

Buckle Up America
www.buckleupamerica.org

This site is the online headquarters of a national organization which works, in coordination with the National Highway Traffic Safety Administration, to promote the proper use of safety belts and child safety seats.

CARFAX

www.carfax.com

Since 1986, CARFAX has provided Vehicle History Reports on specific makes and models of cars in order to help people make informed decisions when buying a used car.

Coalition Against Insurance Fraud

insurancefraud.org

Founded in 1993, the Coalition is a watchdog group that addresses the concerns of consumers, insurance companies, legislators, regulators, and others who may be the victims of fraud.

Green Vehicle Guide

www.epa.gov/greenvehicles

The site, sponsored by the United States Environmental Protection Agency, rates automobiles according to how environmentally friendly they are.

Insure.com

www.insure.com

This site enables people to shop for the best deals in auto, rental, dental, travel, life, health, and home insurance from over 200 companies.

Insurance Institute for Highway Safety (IIHS)

www.highwaysafety.com

The IIHS, financially supported by car insurers, describes itself as an "independent, nonprofit, scientific, and educational organization dedicated to reducing the losses—deaths, injuries, and property damage—from crashes on the nation's highways." The site provides the results of recent crash tests, as well as information about auto theft and accident prevention.

Kids and Cars *www.kidsandcars.org*

Kids in Cars *www.kidsincars.org*

These organizations seek to raise the public awareness about the need for adults and caregivers to ensure the safety of children in and around automobiles. The sites contain statistics about child injuries and fatalities in events involving cars, as well as tips for preventing such events.

National Highway Traffic Safety Administration (NHTSA)

www.nhtsa.dot.gov

Sponsored by the U.S. Department of Transportation, this site provides the latest news about automobile safety, driving and accident statistics, and the results of studies concerning crash tests, child seats, and fuel economy.

Additional Periodical Articles with Abstracts

More information about cars, the automobile industry, and related topics can be found in the following articles. Readers who require a more comprehensive selection are advised to consult the *Readers' Guide to Periodical Literature*, *Readers' Guide Abstracts*, *Social Sciences Abstracts*, and other H.W. Wilson publications.

Cars That Can Save Your Life. Dan Carney. *Better Homes and Gardens*, v. 80 pp86–91 March 2002.

Carney writes that surviving a major auto accident is partly a matter of luck, but certain cars do an excellent job of protecting their occupants. He discusses the results of safety tests conducted by the Insurance Institute for Highway Safety and the U.S. Department of Transportation.

Drive Time. Sonia Alleyne. *Black Enterprise*, v. 34 pp108–10+ November 2003.

Alleyne writes that modern cars can provide almost all the conveniences of home and work. According to the aftermarket trade group Specialty Equipment Market Association, roughly $27 billion has been spent on car enhancements—DVD players, PlayStations, full entertainment systems, VCRs, satellite radio, and TVs in the front and rear—in the aftermarket. Those who install these enhancements are interviewed, and they say their typical clientele range from age 15 to 50. Apart from personalization, Alleyne reports, convenience and comfort are significant factors.

Bush's Nuclear FreedomCAR. Bret Lortie. *The Bulletin of the Atomic Scientists*, v. 60 p12 May/June 2004.

Promoted as a way to reverse U.S. dependence on foreign oil and global warming, the "FreedomCar," Lortie reports, may require the construction of new nuclear power plants, which has not occurred in the United States for decades. In his 2003 State of the Union address, President Bush proposed $1.2 billion to fund research into the car "so that Americans can lead the world in developing clean, hydrogen-powered automobiles." Renewable energy is insufficient for generating the quantity of hydrogen that the world is going to need, says Dan Keuter, vice president of nuclear development for Energy, the second-largest nuclear energy producer in the United States, which hopes to break ground on its cogeneration "Freedom Reactor" within the next five years.

Designer Cars. Gail Edmondson. *Business Week*, pp56–61 February 16, 2004.

According to Edmondson, a 10-year quest to narrow the engineering and quality divide among the world's carmakers has forced companies to compete on appearance. By developing a vehicle that is aesthetically pleasing, manufacturers can add up to 1 percent to the sticker price and still outperform their competitors. To help them achieve this, Edmondson writes, the industry's biggest players are taking on more staff, investing millions in high-tech studios, and paying higher amounts to employ star designers, often luring them from other firms. Designers claim that companies such as GM and Ford have increased the amount they spend on design by at least 50 percent since the early 1990s. Booz Allen Hamilton estimates that leading car designers can earn almost $1 million in salary and bonuses.

Quandary at the Rental Counter. Pallavi Gogoi. *Business Week*, p140 July 15, 2002.

Gogoi reports that many people who rent cars feel obliged to take out extra insurance offered by the rental company. The coverage is outrageously expensive, Gogoi writes, but one out of five renters takes at least some of it, according to a recent study by Progressive, because they are concerned that they would not be protected otherwise. People with full insurance on their own cars, Gogoi explains, are typically covered for the same damages in rental cars but should consult their insurance agent first because coverage can vary between states. Advice is provided on whether or not to take out extra insurance on a rental car.

The Smell of Diesel Is Back in the Air. Christine Tierney. *Business Week*, p72 May 12, 2003.

According to Tierney, two German-based car companies are preparing to offer U.S. buyers versions of popular models with new, high-mileage diesel engines that are much improved on those of a generation ago. Volkswagen will introduce a diesel Passat in fall 2003, while Mercedes-Benz will introduce a diesel E-Class in 2004. These models are currently popular in Europe, where diesel accounts for 40 percent of the auto market, but, Tierney writes, the Germans will have a difficult job convincing Americans that they should think again about diesel.

Battle of the Neither-Nors. Tony Swan. *Car and Driver*, v. 48 pp92–95+ April 2003.

Swan defines crossover vehicles as those that defy traditional classification and include a bewildering variety of machines. A comparison test involving a 600-mile midwinter ramble to northern Michigan ranks the all-around usefulness of five crossover vehicles that resemble SUVs, with some extra ground clearance and cargo- and passenger-carrying flexibility; are conceived to deliver carlike drivability; and are closely grouped in the low-luxury $33,000–$35,000 range: the Honda

Pilot EX, Nissan Murano SE AWD, Toyota Highlander Limited V-6 4WD, Mitsubishi Endeavor Limited AWD, and Buick Rendezvous CXL Versatrak AWD.

The Buyers Have Spoken: Forget Electric Cars. Patrick Bedard. *Car and Driver*, v. 49 p26 January 2004.

Bedard discusses the lack of interest in Toyota's RAV4 EV, a battery-powered electric SUV with a range of between 80 and 100 miles between charges. A California-only program allowed prospective customers to try the vehicle after making a tentative commitment via the Internet, an idea similar to something the company had already done with the Prius hybrid vehicle. Nonetheless, just 213 RAV4 EVs were sold in the six months before Toyota terminated the program, compared with sales of 3,262 for the Prius during its first six months. Toyota concluded, as had General Motors before it, that there was no possibility of making profits from electric cars.

ForMore ForUs. Ray Hutton. *Car and Driver*, v. 49 p39 May 2004.

The cute two-seat urban runabout from Mercedes is making its way slowly to America, Hutton says. The first Smart car to be sold in the United States will be small by American standards but not tiny like the original car, which its manufacturer imagined could be parked perpendicular to the curb rather than parallel. The Smart car to be launched in America will be a five seat, four wheel-drive quasi-SUV rival for the Toyota RAV4, the Honda CR-V, and a range of upcoming potential small wagons from Audi, BMW, and Mercedes. At first, in 2006, the company will have only one product to sell, however: the ForMore, a physically bigger vehicle that is likely to come with a 1.8- or 2.0-liter Mitsubishi engine.

Cars Should Be Made Safer for Children. *Consumer Reports*, v. 68 p57 October 2003.

The writer discusses how the Consumers Union is urging the auto industry, Congress, and the National Highway Traffic Safety Administration to give serious consideration to technologies that are being developed, or already exist, to make vehicles safer for children. He also describes the advantages of a number of these technologies—backup warning devices, power-window devices, and child car seats.

Fuel Economy Stalled in Traffic. *Consumer Reports*, v. 67 pp56–59 December 2002.

The article explains that American consumers are concerned about the fuel economy issue. In 2000 J. D. Power and Associates, a marketing information-services firm that regularly polls vehicle owners, found that close to 60 percent of respondents to its annual survey of new-car owners rated fuel economy "extremely important," in contrast to the 40 percent ratings documented from 1996 through 1999. The factors driving consumer worries, the article says, are global warming, unrest in the Middle East, gasoline prices, and excess consumption. The growing number of large, fuel-hungry sports utility vehicles and trucks means that the average overall fuel economy of all new vehicles in the United States is at its lowest point in 22 years. The writer discusses the main options for enhanced fuel-saving.

Child Restraints: How Can They Be Improved? *Consumers' Research Magazine*, v. 86 pp28–29 July 2003.

The article reports that new study of almost 100 crashes in which children riding in restraints died discovered that many fatal crashes involving child occupants were so severe that enhanced child restraints would not have prevented the fatalities. In excerpts from a conversation, Chris Sherwood, research scientist at the University of Virginia's Automobile Safety Laboratory and lead author of the research report, discusses the findings.

Injuries, Collisions, and Thefts—How Autos Fare. *Consumers' Research Magazine*, v. 86 pp23–25 December 2003.

A table, reprinted from a report by the Highway Loss Data Institute, presents data that summarize the recent insurance injury, collision, and theft losses of passenger cars, pickup trucks, and utility vehicles based on the loss experience of 2000–2 models from their first sales through May 2003. An analysis of the data is included.

Driving Clean. Jim Motavalli. *E: The Environmental Magazine*. v. 15 pp23–25 January/February 2004.

According to Motavalli, auto companies are concerned about a small California state agency known as the Air Resources Board (ARB), which sets the state's emissions policy. ARB's strict clean air rules have effectively compelled the auto industry to produce new generations of low-emission vehicles. The auto industry, Motavalli writes, hates ARB and has attempted to circumvent its rules through litigation. Nonetheless, the automakers dropped their lawsuits when ARB modified its regulations to give the companies credit for the production of environmentally responsible versions of ordinary gasoline cars known as PZEVs (partial zero-emission vehicles). Some industry observers contend that PZEVs are as environmentally friendly as battery cars.

Sporty Inefficiency. *Environment*, v. 43 p4 December 2001.

This article argues that the fuel efficiency of SUVs should be improved. As SUVs are considered light trucks, they do not have to be as efficient as cars. Although the light truck category used to apply to vehicles used to haul materials for farming or construction, today half of the new vehicles sold are light trucks and are usually not used to haul anything. According to the Sierra Club, auto companies such as Ford could make SUVs more efficient without sacrificing performance. By doing so, a truck like the Explorer would release 43 percent less global-warming pollution.

The Disposal Car. Jonathan Fahey. *Forbes*, v. 173 p68 May 24, 2004.

Fahey writes that owners of expensive cars are increasingly finding that air bags and high-tech, high-cost parts make it cheaper to replace the whole car after a crash. According to the trade magazine Collision Repair Industry Insight, the percentage of cars totaled by insurance firms after a crash increased from 8 percent in 1992 to 16 percent in 2003; insurance companies generally will not fix a car if repairs cost over 65 percent of the value of the vehicle. Fahey reports on the high cost of replacing such items as air bags, headlight assemblies, and aluminum structural parts.

Too Much Globalism. Jerry Flint. *Forbes*, v. 171 p96 February 17, 2003.

Flint discusses the drive for lower costs that leads U.S. auto manufacturers to relocate abroad. Nevertheless, he says, the most successful vehicle producers are foreign companies expanding their operations in the United States. These companies avoid protectionism, obtain immense subsidies from Southern states for their plants, and although they pay Detroit wage scales, have nonunion employees who are younger, do not achieve the top rates, and are not yet receiving pensions. According to Flint, the experience of foreign manufacturers can teach Detroit that quality is most important, not where the vehicle is made or what the labor costs are, and that Americans will pay more for a vehicle if they believe it is better.

Caution: Pollution Ahead. Kelly Sims Gallagher. *Foreign Policy*, p12 January/February 2003.

Gallagher, a research fellow at the Energy Technology Innovation Project at the Belfer Center for Science and International Affairs at Harvard University, responds to the article "China's Car Bomb," which appeared in the September–October 2002 issue. She notes that the article appropriately focuses on the imminent head-on collision between car usage and air pollution in China but says that the claim that Chinese decision makers do not have much concern for environmental fallout is too simplistic and unfair.

China's Car Bomb. *Foreign Policy*, pp14–15 September/October 2002.

This article explains that economists predict the size of China's auto industry will rival that of North America by 2025, but with urban pollution already out of control, China could be heading for disaster. Chinese authorities have set an explicit goal of one vehicle for every family, but according to the Stockholm Environment Institute and the United Nations Development Programme's *2002 China Development Report*, Chinese decision makers seem fascinated by cars as "symbols of modernization" with little concern for environmental fallout. Levels of air pollution in China are already some of the worst ever recorded, and the World Bank reports that 16 of the world's 20 most polluted cities are in China. In spite of this, the article claims, most Chinese cities do not actively promote even basic emission standards.

Detroit Buffs Up. Alex Taylor, 3d. *Fortune*, v. 149 pp90–92+ February 9, 2004.

With the launch of new models, according to Taylor, U.S. automakers are displaying a passion for winning customers that they have not shown in years. Having lost another 1.5 percentage points of the domestic market to foreign competitors in 2003, Detroit now accounts for only 60.2 percent of vehicles sold in the United States, the lowest percentage ever. In 2004, Taylor says, GM, Ford, and Daimler-Chrysler will pull out all the stops and unveil a record 48 new or revised sedans, coupes, minivans, sports cars, sport utility vehicles, crossovers, and pickups. Although the companies' reputation among consumers for making dull cars will not be reversed in a year, Taylor argues, at least Detroit is attempting to compete with foreign makers.

Dude, Where's My Hybrid? Stuart F. Brown. *Fortune*, v. 147 pp112–14+ April 28, 2003.

Brown reports on Detroit's impending entries in the budding market of hybrid vehicles. Americans surprised the auto industry by purchasing 36,000 Toyota and Honda hybrids in 2002, a number that is predicted to rise to some 58,000 in 2003, says research firm J. D. Power and Associates. Seen as a percentage of total U.S. vehicle sales, Brown says, the impact of hybrids so far is small, comprising only 0.2 percent of the market in 2002, but such growth is difficult to dismiss, so General Motors, Ford, and DaimlerChrysler are working with varying levels of urgency to produce their own hybrid models. The writer discusses the design, operation, and advantages of hybrids.

Our Mutual Ford: Cities Embrace Car Sharing. Michele Mariani. *Governing*, v. 15 pp36+ June 2002.

According to Mariani, increasing congestion and pollution in big cities has made the concept of car sharing more attractive. Roughly a dozen cities across the United States operate car-sharing systems, which combine the primary use of public transportation with short-term car rentals for trips beyond transit lines. Numerous challenges remain, however, the biggest of which is familiarizing people with the concept and then persuading them to use it. Car-sharing companies, Mariani writes, must demonstrate the convenience of reserving, driving, and parking the cars, so that car owners will become car sharers.

The Teenage Highway Slowdown. Alan Ehrenhalt. *Governing*, v. 15 pp4–6 March 2002.

Ehrenhalt discusses graduated licensing laws, under which young novice drivers move in stages from highly restricted learner permits to full adult privileges. Instituted in the mid-1990s, more than 40 states have graduated licensing in one form or another. The laws differ, but there are three basic components. One is a period in which teenage drivers can drive only with adult accompaniment; second is nighttime curfew time, after which they cannot drive at all; and third is a limit on the number of passengers they are permitted to carry. Eherenhalt quotes statistics compiled by the Insurance Institute for Highway Safety indicating the successful reduction of teenage road deaths in states that adopt graduated licensing, but he argues that parents are the main obstacle to safer licensing laws.

Is It Time to Get off the Road? *Harvard Health Letter*, v. 27 pp1–3 June 2002.

This article reports that older drivers are among the most accident-prone groups on the road. According to a study done last year by Johns Hopkins researchers for the Insurance Institute for Highway Safety, such statistics as accidents per vehicle-miles-traveled begin to climb at age 70 and increase further when people get into their 80s. Nineteen states have tightened rules for older drivers, but using age as a screen for winnowing out bad drivers is imprecise, the article claims. Some experts believe that targeted assessments would be more effective.

Time to Reshop. Kimberly Lankford. *Kiplinger's Personal Finance*, v. 57 p89 February 2003.

Lankford offers advice on avoiding substantial increases in auto-insurance payments.

Cool Cars. Charlie Gillis. *Maclean's*, v. 116 pp32–37 September 29, 2003.

Gillis writes that buyers of hybrid-power cars represent a broad shift in the auto marketplace. Since the Toyota Prius debuted in North America four years ago, it has been a favorite of many image-conscious drivers who flaunt the $30,000 hybrid with a gasoline-electric engine as a badge of environmental responsibility. Other cars reflecting a market shift in how vehicles must look, feel, and perform, Gillis explains, include "crossovers," which are amalgams of sports utility vehicles and minivans. According to Gillis, reasons for the shift in the market in Canada include an increase in the average age of vehicle buyers and a large growth in disposable income.

Uh, Rethink That Rebate. Lawrence Ulrich. *Money*, v. 32 p199 December 2003.

Ulrich explains how automobile discounts can damage the resale value of new cars. It is no coincidence, he claims, that General Motors, Ford, and Chrysler are discounting the average vehicle by $3,600, in contrast to $1,750 for European automakers and just $950 for Japanese brands. Resale values for the major U.S. makers' three-year-old models have dropped to 39 percent of the sticker price, down from 45 percent a year ago, according to the latest data from Automotive Lease Guide. According to Ulrich, the bigger the discount, the louder the market is saying that the model was overpriced to start with

Shared Platforms: Smart Business or Vehicular Shell Game? Matt Stone. *Motor Trend*, v. 56 pp32+ June 2004.

Shared vehicle platforms offer manufacturers benefits but also have their down-sides, Stone explains. The idea is to build one car, make variations of it, and market it under different brand names to unique audiences, the aim being to improve production efficiencies, save large amounts of money, and boost profits. When it is carried out well, several aspects of a given architecture or platform can be massaged to meet the need at hand. Stone argues that sharing certain components and gaining economies of scale where possible make for smart manufacturing and good business, although the end result should be legitimately different in order to motivate the buyer.

Oil Smear. William F. Buckley Jr. *National Review*, v. 54 p56 December 9, 2002.

Buckley argues that the anti-SUV ad campaign draws its force from the erroneous environmentalist accusation that Americans use energy recklessly and profli-gately. The authors of the series of advertisements, which are aimed at persuad-ing Americans that the SUV is the true cause of terrorism, are opposed to Americans using oil. Nonetheless, Americans, who number 280 million of the total 6 billion people on the planet, produce almost 25 percent of its goods and services and use 42 percent less energy for each additional dollar of output than was achieved just 30 years ago. Moreover, Buckley asserts, the ways that Americans use their energy are increasingly protective of the environment.

Power Trip. Martin Peretz. *The New Republic*, v. 226 p42 June 17, 2002.

The writer argues that driving a hybrid car, such as the Toyota Pirus, is any American's patriotic duty because it helps loosen Saudi Arabia's stranglehold over U.S. foreign policy.

Pixels to Pavement. Keith Naughton. *Newsweek*, v. 141 pp46–48 March 10, 2003.

Naughton explains that car manufacturers, desperate to connect with Generation Y, are looking for inspiration from video games. Gamers have the demographics—18- to 35-year-old men with disposable income—coveted by carmakers, who have struggled with recent "youth models" and are having a tough time connecting with kids. Games such as Sony's *Gran Turismo 3* (GT3) and Electronic Arts' *Need for Speed*, Naughton writes, are turning millions of boys into living-room racers and becoming the new virtual showroom and design studio for automakers. Mazda, for example, tried to create a buzz for its revived RX sports car by releasing it in pixel form in GT3, two years before the real car debuted.

Big and Bad: SUVs and the Safety Issue. Malcolm Gladwell. *The New Yorker*, v. 79 pp28–33 January 12, 2004.

SUV buyers think that big, heavy vehicles are safe, whereas the benefits of being nimble are in many cases greater than the benefits of being big. Feeling safe has become more important than really being safe in the automobile world. In fact, if consumers really want something big, heavy, and comforting, they should buy minivans, because minivans, with their unit-body construction, do much better in accidents than SUVs. The writer examines how the SUV industry promoted the association of its vehicles with the idea of safety.

Big and Fancy, More Pickups Displace Cars. Danny Hakim. *The New York Times*, ppA1+ July 31, 2003.

Sales of big pickup trucks, which can cost $40,000 and up, have been soaring for several years, Hakim writes. But, he says, the trend toward bigger-than-ever pickups has broad implications for the safety of American drivers, the environment, oil consumption, and the financial health of the auto industry.

Here Come the Discountmobiles. Ted C. Fishman. *The New York Times Magazine*, pp68-70 September 28, 2003.

When China establishes a hyperefficient industrial infrastructure that will enable it to slash car prices, according to Fishman, Chinese cars that will have a significant impact on the low-end car market will arrive in the United States. Paul Lienert, whose *Global Auto Insider* newsletter often alerts Detroit to China's growing critical mass and capabilities in the car industry, sees the Chinese exporting a car with plenty of Western technology to North America within the next five years and offering cars that some Americans will find acceptable for $6,000 or $7,000.

Is Your Child's Car Seat Safe? Jessica Snyder Sachs. *Parenting*, v. 16 pp135–36+ October 2002.

According to experts, Sachs reports, most infants and children in the United States ride in cars without adequate protection. More than 1.5 million children are involved in car crashes each year in the United States; more than 2,000 of these die, and over 30,000 are seriously injured. Sachs writes that the vast majority of state regulations fall far short of federal and professional recommendations despite recent and continuing improvements. Advice is provided on buying the right car seat for children according to age and weight and on using it correctly.

Car H2.0, Where Are You? Eric Adams. *Popular Science*, v. 264 pp130–31 May 2004.

Adams reports on the flood of modern global positioning systems (GPS) navigation systems for automobiles on the market today. Although a GPS device is probably unnecessary for day-to-day life, he says, automotive navigation will make even the occasional road trip considerably easier for drivers who visit new places with any regularity. Four types of GPS navigation systems for automobiles are described, and advice on purchasing and using these systems is provided.

Coast to Coast on a Single Tank? Trevor Thieme. *Popular Science*, v. 261 pp87–88 August 2002.

Thieme discusses a prototype for a car its inventors claim will drive coast to coast on the equivalent of one SUV's tank of gas. Doug Malewicki and Len Stobar created the three wheeled C2C, which will weigh less than 600 pounds, without corporate backing. Thieme points out that high mileage vehicles are frequently associated with unacceptably slow speeds or require pristine test-track conditions to achieve top mpg. However, according to Malewicki, the C2C will cruise at 70 mph. A proof-of-concept trip is planned for May 2003.

Buckle Up—The Right Way. Julia Van Tine. *Prevention*, v. 52 p52 October 2000.

Researchers from the University of Pennsylvania and Children's Hospital, Philadelphia, and State Farm Insurance Companies claim that children may not be protected from injuries in a car accident if they are not restrained correctly for their age and size, writes Van Tine. Car-safety experts in an ongoing study found that 83 percent of children ages four to eight were strapped into ill-fitting adult seat belts too soon. Furthermore, 30 percent of babies under one year rode facing forward. Both mistakes could cause concussions and more serious injuries in a crash.

Clean Machines. Andy Simmons and Richard Sacks. *Reader's Digest.* v. 164 pp81–83 April 2004.

Simmons and Sacks present viable alternatives to the traditional gasoline-fueled car. Motor vehicles produce more than 1.6 billion tons of pollutants annually, they write, and the United States imports 55 percent of its oil at a cost of $200,000 a minute. Many alternative fuels provide better mileage and less pollution and can lead to savings and substantial tax breaks. While energy companies will not build alternative fuel stations until demand rises, the writers point out, consumers will not buy the cars if they cannot fuel them.

The SUV on the Couch: Interview with C. Rapaille. Erik Hedegaard. *Rolling Stone*, p82 November 13, 2003.

Hedegaard presents an interview with psychologist Clotaire Rapaille, who gathers consumers in darkened rooms where they reveal how various features in a car make them feel. Topics discussed include the reactions of Detroit to his theories.

Getting Back at Mother Nature. Catherine M. Roach. *Sierra*, v. 87 p84 May/June 2002.

Roach argues that automobile ads often praise the same gorgeous natural landscapes that unfettered driving endangers. Nature can remind people of their limitations as physical beings in a world they cannot fully control, but the ads suggest that a vehicle will provide both freedom from nature and the freedom of nature. Such ads encourage people to dismiss ecological knowledge of their dependence on a healthy environment, Roach says, and any motivation for environmental protection is undermined.

Building a Safer Driver. Peter Dizikes. *Technology Review*, v. 106 pp20–21 October 2003.

Some car manufacturers intend to install more-sophisticated driver-warning systems, Dizikes reports. Unlike previous safety improvements—such as air bags or antilock brakes—that increase the car's ability to protect drivers and passengers from accidents, these new technologies are designed to help avoid accidents in the first place. Such features, Dizikes says, including radar- and video-based safety devices that warn the driver when the car veers over lane markings or too close to other vehicles, could add cost-effective marketing allure as well as safety. In the next few years, Dizikes claims, the new safety systems will probably trickle into showrooms even without new federal guidelines.

Baby, You Can Drive My Car. Daren Fonda. *Time*, v. 161 pp46–48 June 30, 2003.

Fonda writes that car manufacturers are chasing the young with models like the new Toyota Scion, aimed at recent college graduates who desire an affordable, functional vehicle. Other manufacturers are attempting to make their existing youth cars more attractive by filling them with higher-performance engines and hot-rod accessories. Generation Y, the 68 million Americans born between 1977 and 1995 that represent the biggest demographic bulge since that of their boomer parents, will drive car sales over the next 20 years, Fonda says. Automakers are clamoring to supply the first new car to these young people in the hope that they will develop a brand loyalty later in life.

Why Hybrids Are Hot. Anita Hamilton. *Time*, v. 159 pp52–3 April 29, 2002.

Hamilton explains that the auto industry is having another go at hybrid cars. The first generation of hybrids—cars that run on gas and electricity—barely dented the consciousness of the car-buying American public: Only 20,000 of the 17 million automobiles sold in the United States in 2001 were hybrids. A hybrid version of the Honda Civic, America's best-selling compact car, recently hit the dealerships. Next year Ford is expected to be the first U.S. automaker to introduce a hybrid vehicle, with Toyota, General Motors, and Chrysler promising a new selection of hybrid vehicles by 2004. J. D. Power and Associates, which studies consumer auto buying trends, expects that by 2006, American consumers will be buying half a million hybrids a year.

Attack of the Four-Wheeled Giants: SUVs. Peter J. Cooper. *USA Today Magazine*, v. 132 pp66–68 March 2004.

Cooper argues that the remedy to the problem of the proliferation of SUVs is to encourage a more receptive, responsible, and nonelitist attitude in the minds of SUV owners. SUVs cause the death of several thousand people in the United States every year, Cooper writes, yet many SUV owners are seemingly still unaware, unconvinced, or uncaring of the injury these "safe" rolling fortresses can inflict upon themselves and other people. Moreover, he asserts, a childish "I'm bigger than you are" mentality exists among some SUV drivers, whose driving techniques sometimes suggest a desire to overpower smaller vehicles. A reduction in the number of SUVs on public thoroughfares would improve a significant aspect of the American quality of life, Cooper argues.

No Place to Hide. Richard J. Newman. *U.S. News & World Report*, v. 135 pp32–33 July 14, 2003.

Technology is beginning to throw new light on the causes of automobile accidents, Newman says. Practically every new car sold today contains an event data recorder, which stores key information such as the car's speed, deceleration, or seat-belt use once sensors detect a collision. Most automakers encrypt the data, writes Newman, but General Motors and Ford are allowing the statistics on their cars to be retrieved by mechanics or crash investigators with a simple handheld device. Toyota and others are expected to follow suit. Already, the data are being used in court cases and insurance investigations, bringing new tradeoffs between auto safety and individual privacy.

Land of the Free—Parking: The Pay Lot Could Be the Key to Our Energy Future. Alan Durning. *Utne Reader*, pp26–29 September/October 2001.

According to Durning, free parking is a major cause of America's insatiable thirst for gasoline and automobile use. As a nation, we pay more to store our vehicles during the 23 hours a day when they are not in use than we do to keep their tanks full. Fifty percent of the cost of parking is paid by employers, businesses, and tax-payers, and another 40 percent is paid through rent and mortgages for off-street parking at home. Durning discusses why pay parking is rare outside the center of large cities and claims that complementary parking encourages workers and cus-tomers to drive and discourages the use of mass transit, a bike, or pedestrian travel. The demand for gasoline and automobile use drives a range of national concerns: rising fuel prices, global climate change, reliance on foreign oil, tighten-ing traffic snarls, relentless sprawl, and worsening urban smog.

Erasing Boundaries. Peter S. Hellman. *Vital Speeches of the Day*, v. 64 pp57–60 November 1, 1997.

In an address to the University of Michigan Management Briefing Seminars, Traverse City, Michigan, the president and CEO of TRW Inc. discusses globaliza-tion in the automobile industry. Globalization, he says, is an opportunity for pros-perity and can be a force for positive change if managed skillfully. Existing auto markets in the world's major economies are growing today at a moderate pace, but nations and regions around the world that are moving toward fully industrial-ized status provide the industry with a market that will grow much faster for many decades to come. That demand will double the industry's total global poten-tial for growth, he argues, but efficiency will be required as a means of enlarging and accelerating earnings.

Monster Truck Rally: Defending the SUV. Zachary Roth. *The Washington Monthly*, v. 35 pp13–14 December 2003.

Roth explains that the Sport Utility Vehicle Owners of America (SUVOA) in Washington, D.C., is attempting to defend the SUV. Over the past few years, envi-ronmentalists have criticized the SUV's very low gas mileage, and consumer safety advocates have highlighted the vehicle's disproportionate tendency to kill the drivers of cars with which they collide. Operated by Ron DeFore and Jason Vines, SUVOA has headquarters in the offices of Stratacomm, a very successful Beltway public-relations firm specializing in issues affecting the auto industry. One of the pair's favorite themes, writes Roth, is the anti-SUV "misinformation" and "bias" of the mainstream media, which, Vines says, are leading Americans to drive unsafe cars.

Beast on Wheels: Designing a Car Like a Living Thing. Dick Morley. *Wired*, v. 12 pp116–17 February 2004.

The writer considers how a car would work if it were designed like a living being—as a collection of components wired to regulate one another in response to external stimuli in a similar manner to the way in which organs are mediated by a nervous system. A diagram illustrates the design features of such an organic car.

Index